CRAIG HAZEN

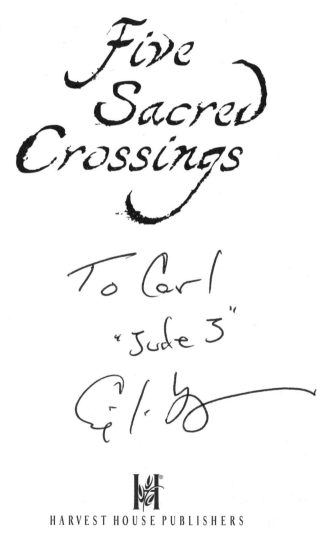

Five Sacred Crossings

To Carl

" Jude 3 "

HARVEST HOUSE PUBLISHERS

EUGENE, OREGON

Craig J. Hazen: This work is published in association with the Conversant Media Group, P.O. Box 3006, Redmond, WA, 98007.

ConversantLife.com is a trademark of the Conversant Media Group. Harvest House Publishers, Inc., is a licensee of the trademark ConversantLife.com.

Photo of The Return of the Prodigal Son by Rembrandt Harmensz van Rijn © SuperStock, Inc. / SuperStock

Cover by Abris, Veneta, Oregon

This is a work of fiction. Names, characters, places, and incidents are products of the author's imagination or are used fictitiously. Any resemblance to actual persons, living or dead, or to events or locales, is entirely coincidental.

FIVE SACRED CROSSINGS
Copyright © 2008 by Craig J. Hazen
Published by Harvest House Publishers
Eugene, Oregon 97402
www.harvesthousepublishers.com

Hazen, Craig James.
Five sacred crossings / Craig J. Hazen.
p. cm.
ISBN-13: 978-0-7369-2196-1 (pbk.)
ISBN-10: 0-7369-2196-6
I. Title
PS3608.A9887F58 2008
813.'6—dc22

2007028422

Printed in the United States of America

08 09 10 11 12 13 14 15 16 / VP-SK / 11 10 9 8 7 6 5 4 3 2 1

Craig Hazen is part of a faith-based online community called ConversantLife.com. At this website, people engage their faith in entertainment, creative arts, science and technology, global concerns, and other culturally relevant topics. While you're reading this book, or after you have finished reading, go to www.conversantlife .com/craighazen and use these icons to read and download additional material from Craig that is related to the book.

Resources: Download study guide materials for personal devotions or a small-group Bible study.

Videos: Click on this icon for interviews and video clips on various topics.

Blogs: Read through blogs and articles and comment on them.

Podcasts: Stream ConversantLife.com podcasts and audio clips.

conversant life .com

engage your faith

For Karen,
who draws all who know her
closer to the Fifth Crossing

Acknowledgments

I must thank several dear friends who assisted, encouraged, and cheered me along the way. J.P. Moreland is one of the most gifted academic cheerleaders I've ever encountered, and I don't know where I'd be professionally or personally without his friendship. John Mark Reynolds likewise was always there with a kind word of counsel and support. Bruce Bickel and Stan Jantz took a risk in opening the door for me to attempt a work of didactic fiction, and Stan's comments on the first draft were very helpful and encouraging. For that I am grateful. The careful reading by Terry Glaspey and Gene Skinner of Harvest House was incredibly valuable. My staff and co-laborers in the apologetics offices at Biola University, Rebecca, Jimmy, and Abigail, eased my insecurities about writing fiction with their enthusiasm for the story, as did my friend Beth Issler. Of course, I am most thankful for my wife, Karen, and our children, Kent, Garrett, Danika, and Maggie. They read the manuscript, gave their input, and provided me with the time to see this project come to fruition.

A Note from the Author

WE WOULD ALL LIKE ANSWERS for life's foundational questions. What kind of meaning can we find in our existence? Does God exist? Can anyone properly claim to have absolute truth? Are all religions basically the same? Is humankind in need of salvation, and if so, what would that salvation look like? Why do we experience evil and suffering in the world? What role does reason play in a religious journey? And so on.

We can easily get discouraged when we talk to friends, family, and neighbors about such things or hear teachers, celebrities, and scholars air their opinions. With so many different answers floating around, we can be tempted to throw up our hands and conclude that even if answers to the most profound questions do exist, we simply have no way to know what those answers are with any authority or clarity.

But we should not lose heart because of the widespread confusion about these issues. If we approach these questions properly, we can find reasonable, persuasive, and satisfying answers. Very often, though, those with the best answers use academic jargon. So even if answers are available, only a few people have immediate access to them.

The field of Christian apologetics has often found itself in this predicament—having reasonable answers but without the language and context to resonate with most people where they are. Apologetics is the Christian discipline that offers reasons for believing the core gospel message and the biblical view of the world. Apologetics has been a central element in Judeo-Christian writings, and the prophets and apostles used it very effectively. The apostle Peter encourages his readers to defend the faith: "Always be prepared to give an answer [the Greek word is *apologian*] to everyone who asks you to give the reason for the hope that you have" (1 Peter 3:15).

In Christian history, almost every generation has offered various "apologies" or defenses to help answer objections to the traditional Christian views on God, man, sin, and salvation. But these defenses usually come from believing theologians, philosophers, lawyers, and scholars of various stripes, often in difficult, technical language. From time to time, however, scholars who are fascinated by presenting reasons for faith have used allegories, analogies, novels, and other modes of storytelling to make specific points about the truth of the Christian view of the world. Many names come to mind, but one that almost everyone is familiar with is the British scholar and author C.S. Lewis, who in the mid-twentieth century wrote such classics as *Mere Christianity, The Chronicles of Narnia, The Great Divorce, The Screwtape Letters,* and many more.

This present work certainly does not in any way compare to what Lewis produced except that it fits in the same category of literature. *Five Sacred Crossings* is a story that provides compelling answers (or at least sketches of such answers) to some of the big questions of life.

This is a story about a man named Dr. Michael Jernigan and his experiences with the mountain people of Cambodia and a group of curious college students in Southern California. This novel communicates real truths about the most important religious questions that human beings ask. Although the story is fictional, it is not at all far-fetched because I based much of it on real-life encounters I have had in secular college classrooms around the world. The ancient text I refer to in the story as *The Five Crossings,* however, does not actually exist.

I hope the story will be compelling enough to entice readers to consider some thoughtful answers to real religious questions—readers who may never read an apologetics textbook. I also hope that you will enjoy the story because if the story brings you any measure of joy, much of the work of apologetics has already been done. As C.S. Lewis pointed out, joy is the "secret signature of each soul." It is an experience that undermines misguided views of the world and drives one to a true foretaste of ultimate reality.

So enjoy!

ONE

MICHAEL JERNIGAN FELT THE EXPLOSION, and every muscle in his body suddenly tensed. Adrenaline flooded his body as a wave of panic gripped him. His mind screamed at him to fall to the floor and get behind cover, but his fifty-six-year-old body was more than a moment or two behind his instincts. His delayed reaction gave him enough time to remember where he was, steady himself, and quickly sit down on the ottoman in front of his reading chair. The blast couldn't have been more than a few blocks away.

His heart kept pounding for a few minutes. He hadn't had a reaction like that for several years—at least not while he was awake. About once a year he still had a flashback from some of his terrifying moments as a nineteen-year-old soldier in Vietnam. Immediately after the war, loud noises of almost any kind triggered his fight-or-flight reaction. Certain sounds, smells, and vibrations transported him back through time to vivid and disturbing memories. As a combat veteran, Michael would never again hear an explosion without jumping. If he had fought any earlier than Vietnam, people would have said he had "shell shock"; now doctors diagnosed him with post-traumatic stress syndrome.

But this was different. It wasn't a trigger experience to a distant memory. This was the real thing.

As Michael's heart began to settle down, he grabbed the

remote control and flipped on the TV to see if he could find a news report about the blast. Nothing yet. *What was it?* He continued to surf the channels to see who might break in first. In the distance, he heard car alarms the concussion had set off. He felt steady enough to go to the window and look out. His corner apartment on the second floor had a decent view in two directions. He actually had an ocean view from his postage-stamp-sized terrace if he leaned over the rail a few feet to look between the two buildings across the street. Seeing no smoke, he went back inside and anxiously waited for a news report. It was Thursday, just before five in the evening. Plenty of light still.

The phone rang, and Michael tensed up again briefly—still a little sensitive. He let the answering machine pick it up. He muted the television so he could hear the message.

"Dr. Jernigan, this is Megan calling from the office. Sorry to bother you on sabbatical, but hey, you only have a few weeks left, don't you? Oh, maybe I shouldn't have said that. Hope that didn't depress you. Well anyway, a friend of yours called from Laguna City College about lecturing in her class for a few weeks starting tomorrow. She said you would know why, and that it's a girl. She'll send you an e-mail with details. Call me if you need anything. Bye."

Michael smiled—he did know what it was about. His friend, Professor Willa Lightner, told him she was going to have a baby and was planning the timing so that she would deliver right after final exam week. She was a good young scholar who managed her classroom and research projects with tight control. Perhaps she thought she could manage a baby the same way. Although Michael had no children of his own, he knew that babies weren't quite as predictable as Willa and her female partner might have hoped. He saw the pregnant Willa two months before and offered to help out if the plan didn't come off as expected. Obviously, such an outcome had never entered Willa's mind.

Willa and Michael spent time together two or three times a year at academic conferences and talked on the phone once in a while in between. They both taught courses in general religious studies and both had specialties in Buddhist studies. Michael was an expert in

South Asian Buddhism and Buddhist history, and Willa studied expressions of Buddhism in contemporary North America. They were often invited to be on panels together at various scholarly gatherings.

Thinking about Willa and her new baby helped settle Michael's body and mind. He still couldn't find any news about the blast, but he could hear sirens approaching. He was already thinking about what Willa might have him cover in the last few weeks of her world religions survey course.

He was also thinking about the strange nature of their friendship. Their shared interest in Buddhism and religious studies was about all they had in common. Willa was a high-energy intellectual who could keep her focus on tasks, despite her lifelong ADHD, by what seemed sheer force of will. Thirty-seven years old, she was nineteen years Michael's junior. She and her female partner, Frieda, had been together since graduate school and finally decided to have a baby by means of artificial insemination. They actually tossed a coin to see who would carry the child. Willa won the toss, and in terms of physical strength for carrying and delivering, she was the right one. She was smaller but made up for her size in strength and determination. Michael later learned that when Willa went into labor earlier than planned, Frieda drove her to the hospital. Willa, thinking she was further along in the delivery process than she actually was, sprinted a couple hundred yards from the parking structure to the hospital entrance, carrying a good-sized overnight bag and leaving Frieda in the dust, carrying only a small digital video recorder.

In the classroom, Professor Lightner was all business. She loved taking the early-morning classes on the semester schedule and had a reputation among the students as a stimulating but intense lecturer. She always seemed to try to cover too much material and was one of the toughest graders outside the math and science departments.

Dr. Lightner also had a predictable approach for teaching about religion at a public college in southern California. She worked hard to treat all religions fairly and make no judgments about whether one system of belief was better or worse, true or false. Her lectures were almost completely descriptive—painting clear pictures about the history, beliefs, and practices of the great world religious traditions. Every semester, curious students asked her which one of the traditions she thought was closest to the truth or the most attractive to her personally. Willa was very adept at sidestepping the question and, in a very professional way, guiding the discussion in a different direction. She knew her religious preference was a sensitive issue in public classrooms, where she might have a wide range of believers and unbelievers. But during the last month of her pregnancy, her usual diplomatic response unwittingly went out the window, and she surprised her class by answering at length with hair-raising candor.

"That question really betrays a kind of unhealthy Western mind-set that misunderstands the nature of religion," she told one lucky student. "Religion is not about 'truth' or 'best.' Religions are not like football games or *American Idol* competitions, where someone wins a trophy or a record deal. You've got to get this straight before this class ends: All religions are mysteries. Sure, we can know *about* them—their rituals, their teachings, art, history—but we can never know if their core spiritual claims are universally true. At that point it's all about personal belief. You either have faith, or you don't. And if it's all about personal belief or faith, then let's stop this silly quest to discover which is best or true or absolute. There's too much at stake. For God's sake, people are killing each other in the name of their religious views—which for the most part can't even be known. How insane is that? What am I doing bringing a child into this madhouse?"

The class sat stunned as Professor Lightner buried her head in her arms on the podium at the front and sobbed. Her outburst raised all kinds of interesting points for discussion, but of course no student was crazy enough or insensitive enough to ask a follow-up question.

Dr. Michael Jernigan was a study in contrast to Willa Lightner. Michael did not teach at Laguna City College, although he lived only half a mile away. He loved the coast and rented his current apartment—just a short walk from the beach—after his wife died of pancreatic cancer four years earlier. He hadn't remarried. Willa was petite, trim, and always professionally dressed; Michael looked like a tall California version of Columbo. He had thick hair that at one time was red but was now well into the pale and gray shades. Instead of a trademark Columbo trench coat, he wore a navy blue cloth jacket almost every day except in the summer.

Professor Jernigan was a tenured faculty member at San Gabriel College—a thriving Christian institution thirty miles inland. For the past twenty-two years he had worked in the Department of Intercultural Studies, teaching courses on world religions, Asian philosophy, and cross-cultural theology. He was best known on and off campus for his textbook *The Religions of Asia,* which was used around the world and had been translated into six different languages. Michael had a tremendous ability with languages and actually did two of the translations of his textbook himself. When he was in the infantry in Vietnam, he picked up conversational Vietnamese within days of being "in country." His commander made him the company translator, something he hated because he frequently had to interrogate villagers and prisoners.

In many ways, Jernigan was a mixed fit for the conservative San Gabriel campus. On one hand, he loved the open spiritual environment and had recently taken a joint appointment with the new Department of Spiritual Formation, which was dedicated to developing the students' faith and personal transformation. Although he adored languages, books, and ideas, he loved pouring himself into his students and colleagues even more. He was a deeply devoted believer, and those who had close contact with him knew that he was the real deal.

Michael mentored one new faculty member who often said that the man never seemed to be alone with his thoughts. He was in a constant conversation with God about everything. He had a unique ability to challenge his friends vigorously over academic ideas or over issues of personal growth and at the same time make them feel loved and safe. The most spiritually mature students on campus couldn't get enough of him. Michael's office hours were always booked solid, often by students who were not enrolled in his classes.

On the other hand, some faculty members had thought for

years that Michael was very much out of place in the conservative Christian community and hoped he would take one of the other job offers he regularly received. Some colleagues who didn't bother to look too deeply at the content or approach of Michael's Christian life seemed constantly on edge about things he would do and say. For instance, Michael learned a great deal about the discipline of meditation from the Buddhists with whom he interacted for years, and he borrowed some of their techniques to enhance his own meditation on Scripture and his focus on God during prayer. His detractors saw an unholy blending of religious practices where Michael saw an act of redemption—a capturing of a neutral human technique for God's purpose.

Michael also was not very concerned about using the sanctified vocabulary of the Christian subculture. Although he knew the Bible and theology extraordinarily well, he communicated the ideas in new and creative ways, causing some consternation among the few on campus and in local churches for whom "new and creative" usually meant scary and threatening.

However, nothing in Michael's life caused his critics to wonder about the depth of his Christian commitment more than this: He smoked cigarettes. This called into question not only his fitness for a Christian college but also his citizenship in California, and for some on the more eccentric edge of liberal West coast activism, his right to the common air supply.

Michael was raised in Wichita, Kansas, where his parents and almost all his neighbors smoked. When he was in Vietnam he began smoking and was never able to quit. He didn't smoke a lot, and he didn't smoke around other people, but he smoked.

For years he tried everything to quit—nicotine gum, counseling, cold turkey, group prayer sessions—but nothing helped him get over his addiction. He gave up trying to quit after his wife died of cancer. Michael's smoking no longer made him feel like a spiritual failure. In a backhanded way, his frailty in this area made him stronger because he had nowhere to turn but to the grace of God. His weakness reminded him where his real strength was, and it gave him compassion for other people in their struggles and failings.

In his apartment, Michael put down the TV remote for a moment to light a cigarette. The screen suddenly flashed Breaking News, and he frantically picked up the remote again to turn up the volume. The reporter said a unit at a self-storage facility had blown up and had destroyed several other units as well. Local police were on the scene investigating and suspected it had been a meth lab.

With one eye on the television report, Michael heated up some leftover lasagna in the microwave and ate it while standing at the kitchen counter. He continued watching for some time as the on-the-scene reporter repeated the same basic facts again and again because no new information was available. Michael still had too much adrenalin in his body to be comfortable, so he decided to walk it out of his system. Rather than heading for the waterfront as he normally would, he put on his blue jacket and walked toward the scene of the blast. He had used that same storage facility when he moved his things to Laguna after his wife passed away, and he was surprised to find that the blast was on the end of the facility farthest from his apartment. For him to feel it as strongly as he did in his apartment, it must have been much bigger than he first thought. He really couldn't get close. Crime-scene tape surrounded a wide perimeter, and lots of other people had come to see what happened—especially every kid with a skateboard, scooter, or bicycle.

He got close to the crowd, put out his cigarette, and climbed up on a short planter wall just as one of the fire trucks pulled away. This left him with a great view into the middle of the action. If the explosion had started a fire, it was out now, but the blast had taken out at least eight of the storage units.

"Don't look like no meth lab to me," said a young man with no shirt, a lot of tattoos, stringy hair, and a barely visible mustache. Michael just nodded.

"Don't look like nobody's hurt 'cept that guy over there," the young man said while pointing across the street from the storage facility.

Michael looked away from the flashing lights and saw the mangled body of an Irish setter in the gutter.

"Looks like he was throwed twenty yards."

Michael didn't say anything or even nod this time. Since Vietnam, he didn't do well at accident scenes, he didn't watch war movies, and he stayed away from most news reports about war-torn areas. It was all fodder for flashbacks. If he'd had a better sense of the size of the blast, he would have walked toward the beach as usual. But he'd seen enough, and the sky was turning dark. He walked back to his apartment and watched *The Simpsons* on TV and then a couple of mindless sitcoms to get his thoughts off the scene he had just witnessed. That helped a little, but he took a sleeping pill to try to avoid any nightmares over the explosive reminders of his tour in Vietnam. Besides, he needed some sound sleep to be ready for Willa's 8:30 class the next morning.

TWO

THE SUN WAS STILL BURIED well below the hills in the east when Michael got up, and he made some strong coffee to help him regain consciousness. That and a cigarette usually did the trick—but today was different. He was wide awake once he unrolled the morning newspaper and read the huge headline:

Accidental Blast Uncovers
Local Islamic Terror Cell

Michael was stunned. He fixed his eyes on the article while he felt around for the TV remote. He flipped on the tube, and the national morning news shows were all covering the incident. There was still a lot of speculation about the details, but one Indonesian student from Laguna City College had been killed in the blast, and officials were searching for two other Indonesian nationals who were also enrolled at LCC.

Michael was not an expert in radical Islam, but he had been a visiting professor in the Indonesian capital, Jakarta, a year before the September 11 attacks. Even then he had been assigned a special bodyguard by campus security because he was an American citizen and therefore a target. He knew firsthand that the most populous Muslim country on the planet was roiling and would not be dormant for long on the world-terror stage. Though armed with this advanced knowledge, he was still staggered by the morning's news and thankful to God for protecting the innocents.

Talking heads on every cable news outlet were speculating that this incident represented the new tactic in terror: small cells in smaller towns focusing on smaller but more vulnerable targets. Even though only one person died, and that person was one of the alleged conspirators, the seeds of fear were effectively sown—especially in Southern California. The homeland security expert in the sheriff's office admitted to a reporter, probably without checking with his superiors, that more than four hundred individuals were on the terror watch list in Laguna County alone. The expert was dismayed that none of the three suspects was on the list. They were students in good standing, and none attended a local mosque. One was majoring in chemistry and the other two in microbiology—areas of study that could aid terror plans. This added fuel to the fire of cable news discussion.

Michael had to tear himself away from the TV coverage to get dressed, grab Willa's e-mail, and get out the door to campus. He had taught these classes for so many years, he generally didn't bring anything with him—no briefcase, no notes, no books—just his cigarettes and lighter, his reading glasses, and the e-mail printout.

He had been a guest lecturer for Willa in previous semesters, so he knew where her classroom was. Walking in from the parking lot, he read the thorough e-mail Willa had sent from the hospital. It said that the class met on Monday, Wednesday, and Friday. This was Friday—not a great day to start something new with students. When he arrived at the front door to the classroom building he was met by Dr. Marvin Gelman, the new chair of the Department of Religious Studies. Willa had predicted this in her e-mail.

"Professor Jernigan, it's an honor to have you here. Let me show you to the classroom."

They went downstairs to a basement room where bleary-eyed students were beginning to arrive. The room had no windows, and Michael was slightly claustrophobic.

"Funny thing about education. We're supposed to be telling the students about the amazing world that surrounds them, and we often do it in rooms with no windows through which to see it,"

Michael said, mostly as a form of therapy to cope with the closed space he was walking into.

"A little distance from the real world might be a good thing today," said Dr. Gelman.

"Oh yes, what's the reaction on campus so far?" asked Michael.

"I got here at six this morning, and the lights were on in the president's office," Gelman replied. "I assume she and the vice-presidents are working on some kind of statement. I got my first call at three thirty this morning; East Coast news outlets wanting to scare up some expert on campus to interview. Erin Pletcher, our professor of Islamic studies, has been in our conference room with various news crews since five thirty this morning. She's really an expert in birthing rituals among the Druze in Lebanon and Syria, but she seems to be holding her own on questions about Islamic groups in the East Indies."

"Do you think the students will know much about all this yet?" said Michael.

"You can pretty much count on the fact that they didn't read the newspaper or see any TV news," answered Gelman. "Those who check the sports scores or weather report on the Internet probably bumped into the news about it. I'd say half the class slept until twenty minutes ago and haven't heard a thing about it yet. It's eight thirty; shall we get started?"

Michael figured about twenty students were in the classroom, which seated about thirty-five, and a few more students were still rushing in to take seats. He didn't see that very often; students usually drifted into his classes. He said softly to Gelman, "Wow, Willa must get on them if they're late."

Gelman didn't hear Michael; he was already stepping forward to introduce him to the class.

"Good morning. In case you haven't heard, Dr. Lightner's baby has arrived, and she will be out for these last few weeks of class. But she certainly did not leave you in the lurch. She has arranged for a very distinguished substitute. Dr. Michael Jernigan is a professor at San Gabriel College, but you can bet that almost every faculty member here and in religious studies departments around the world has studied and assigned his renowned book on Asian religions—which in my view has the best section on comparative Buddhist philosophy ever written."

Michael was always a little embarrassed during academic introductions that seemed to go over the top. But it was part of the scholarly culture. Indeed, professors don't have résumés that paint a basic job history; instead, they have *curricula vitae* that are supposed to give an account of their "course of life." Some pretension was unavoidable in the academic career path. It was simply the nature of the beast.

"If any of you speaks Vietnamese or Thai, or Icelandic for that matter," continued Gelman, "you might get a special tutorial in that language during his office hours. I first saw Dr. Jernigan at the University of Hawaii at a large conference on the future of religion in the Pacific Rim. He was sharing the stage with the significantly lesser lights of the Dalai Lama and Sita Ram Goel."

Gelman chuckled at his own joke. No one else did.

"Well, let me turn it over to Dr. Jernigan," concluded Gelman.

"Thank you so much for that kind introduction, Dr. Gelman. I don't know how I'm going to live up to all that..."

Gelman was out the door before Michael finished his standard polite response, and he immediately realized Gelman had also raced out before breaking any news to the class about the small matter of fellow students plotting to blow the town up. It didn't seem to Michael like the kind of thing the new guy should be telling the students.

THREE

MICHAEL SAT ON THE EDGE of the teacher's table in the front of class and was about a nanosecond from uttering his first word to the class when a girl in the second row of seats blurted out, "What do you know about those terrorists with the bombs?"

"How many of you know anything about that?" Michael asked.

Only two people raised their hands—the girl who asked the question and the girl sitting right beside her. That was it.

"What's your name?" Michael said to the girl who asked the question.

"Charlene," she said.

"So how did you hear about the alleged terrorists?"

"My mom called me on the way to campus and told me I shouldn't go cuz there were terrorists on campus or something. I'm like, 'I'm sure,' and she says it's totally on the news."

The rest of the students looked at each other, and several whispered conversations ignited among them.

"How do you know about this, Mizz...?" Michael asked, pointing to the other girl who raised her hand.

"Charlene told me," said the girl.

"Her name is Reagan," said Charlene, answering for Reagan, who had missed the subtle inquiry about her name.

Another student sitting in the back of the room, a male with long blond hair, had his hand up. "I totally heard the explosion. We were eating at a pizza place pretty close to it. We ran down the street a couple of blocks, but it was behind the gates of the storage place. My friend said it was probably a meth kitchen going off. He's like, 'Man, if you cook with too much ether or naptha you get a fireball and then you got acid and glass and flames flying everywhere.'"

"And what's your name?" Michael asked.

"Darren Stevens, like the guy in *Bewitched*."

Michael and everyone else in the classroom were a little curious to know how Darren's friend knew so much about illegal drug labs, but Michael didn't go there.

"I heard the blast too, and it startled the daylights out of me," Michael said. "Reporters last night thought it was probably a meth lab too. But this morning they were all reporting that a local terror group was trying to assemble a small bomb and accidentally detonated it. They apparently had enough ingredients to make a truck bomb that could level a city block—like the Oklahoma City bombing—but only a couple handfuls of the stuff went off, and it obliterated eight storage units. One young man was killed and two are on the run."

Michael hesitated for a moment as he saw frightened looks begin to form on a few of the faces in the room.

Charlene charged ahead with the most distressing information, "My mom said they were all students here and that they were going to blow up the campus."

A girl near the back threw her hand over her mouth, and her eyes got wide.

"I haven't heard that reported," said Michael, trying to ease the mounting fear. "I mean, they were students here, but I haven't heard if they were planning anything on campus."

"Do you know their names? I wonder if they were some of those Arabic guys who always sit under that tree outside the library," asked Darren.

"I haven't heard their names yet, but they were Indonesians, not from the Middle East."

Michael took some time to draw a makeshift world map on the whiteboard and explain that Indonesia was a group of islands that formed the dividing line between the South Pacific and the Indian Ocean. He gave a brief history of how this nation had become overwhelmingly Muslim even though it is so far from the sacred sites in Saudi Arabia. Michael was not an expert in global Islam but had taught courses on world religions for years. He also had an almost photographic memory and an encyclopedic knowledge of most things he taught. He rarely brought lecture notes with him to classes or conferences.

"I'd say the odds are about eighty percent that these three Muslim students were connected with *Jemaah Islamiyah,* which is the most militant group in the islands and is linked to al Qaeda. Generally, Islam in this region is fairly moderate. But just like in Turkey, which is also very moderate, some radical factions believe that engaging in *jihad,* or holy war, is a great act of obedience and devotion," Michael explained.

On rare occasion, circumstances out of our control produce extraordinary moments of intense learning. The students were leaning forward in their seats and hanging on every word. They were working out their anxiety by peppering Dr. Jernigan with questions, many of which he couldn't answer. Will the two who escaped come back? Does the Koran teach them to do this? Why are some radical and some not?

The gregarious Charlene waited her turn to ask her pointed question. Showing almost no emotion, she slouched down in her chair, chewing gum, and asked, "Why do they want to kill us?"

Like a group of penguins, all heads in the room were pointed at Charlene, and in unison they turned toward the professor.

"Because their hearts need to be transformed," he said immediately but very softly.

The answer may have surprised the students as much as Charlene's frightening question. After nearly an entire semester with Dr. Lightner, any of them could have predicted her answer, and it would have had to do with something like social marginalization, lack of economic opportunity, or long-standing colonial oppression.

Everyone sat still, silently waiting for him to say more. Michael let the silence seep in so the comment could do its work on them. He often made spiritual statements in the midst of secular environments to get people thinking in a different direction. With fear thick in the air, his comment was now especially powerful.

Michael stood up, closed his eyes, and pictured a familiar Sanskrit text. It had never been translated into English, so he translated and recited it out loud all at once from memory.

> Dangerous views caused by ignorance flourish
>
> They grow into forests of bramble that entangle defiled hearts
>
> Suspicion and slander and violence by those poisoned with anger abounds

He paused a moment then recited two other texts.

> The heart is deceitful above all things and beyond cure. Who can understand it?
>
> Above all else, guard your heart for it is the wellspring of life.

After another moment of lingering silence, he opened his eyes, looked at Charlene, and asked, "Why *shouldn't* they kill us?"

Charlene slid up a little in her chair, surprised. "What do you mean, why *shouldn't* they kill us? You're kidding, right?" she responded.

"No, I think we need to answer that question," Michael answered.

"Because we didn't do anything," offered Reagan, trying to help.

"Have you submitted to Allah? Have you confessed that Muhammad is Allah's prophet?"

"No," said Charlene and Reagan almost together.

"Then you have violated the most fundamental beliefs of Islam. Why shouldn't they kill us?" he asked again.

"What, you're supposed to kill someone because they don't believe the way you do?" Reagan replied, hoping the line of questioning was just rhetorical and wondering how far Dr. Jernigan was going to take it.

"Oh, but what if it's not just a belief? What if they have an accurate understanding of God and his will?" said Michael.

"They can't...they don't...." Reagan was becoming a little agitated.

Michael wisely moved the focus onto someone else. "Darren. How do we know these Indonesian men in our town are wrong about God and his will?"

Darren's surfer look and vocabulary caused his teachers at the college to have low expectations of him. He was actually one of the top students from his high school and attended Stanford his freshman year, hoping to be a philosophy major. He nearly failed all his courses because he was too busy exploring surfing spots up and down the California coast to attend class. His dad said he wouldn't pay for another semester until Darren finished a year at the nearby Laguna City College with straight A's.

"We can't know if they're right about God. No one can," said Darren.

"But if no one can know if they're right about God, how do you know no one can know?" asked Michael, sounding as paradoxical as one of the Buddhist teachers he had spent so much time with.

No one replied, and Michael let the silence linger again for a couple of beats and then said, "Perhaps it's time to empty our cups."

The class gave him a collective look of puzzlement.

Michael continued, "Zen teachers in Japan tell a parable about a very learned man who went to visit a famous spiritual master. The learned man talked a long time about religion as the master listened patiently. The master got up to serve some tea while the learned man continued on and on. The master filled the visitor's cup to the brim and then kept on pouring. The learned man watched the overflowing cup until he could no longer restrain himself.

"'It's overfull, no more can go in!' the learned man blurted out.

"'You are like the cup,' said the master. How can you contain anything I have for you unless you first empty your cup?'"

Michael paused for comments. None were forthcoming.

"We have potential murderers on our doorstep who plan to kill us in the name of Allah, and yet we're completely stymied in terms of a thoughtful response to their ideas and their motivations. We seem to be filled with ways of thinking about religion that are completely impotent and irrelevant. By any measure, we're in desperate need of a fresh start; real learning has almost completely broken down on the world stage. We need to empty our cups and brew a fresh pot of tea."

The students seemed to be excited about what Dr. Jernigan was saying, but many wondered whether they were even understanding him correctly. His message seemed cryptic, but he sounded as if he was going to address some of the issues about religious truth that had been off limits throughout the semester. Most of the students took the class simply because they were curious about religious ideas and practices. But some in the class were spiritual seekers who were kicking the tires of various religions to see if they might like to take one out for a test drive. A thoughtful evaluation from a renowned expert about the deeper questions of truth would be a great way for them to wrap up the semester.

"Counting today, we only have eight class sessions together, and according to my instructions from Dr. Lightner, I can cover whatever I'd like. Well, after spending only a brief time with you under such intense circumstances, I think I know just what that journey should be. Let's try to tackle some of the stickiest and most provocative issues in the study of religion."

The class was genuinely excited about the prospect. The room suddenly seemed to have windows, and a fresh breeze was blowing through at a time in the semester when students begin to tune out.

"So come ready to take a new path on Monday morning. And bring some friends if you'd like; we have some extra seats. It should be stimulating for all of us. I normally end up learning so much from the students that I feel like I should be paying tuition too."

The students took that as a closing statement and began to pack up their notebooks. Without any warning, Charlene asked, "So what religion are you? Buddhist?"

Without missing a beat, Michael said, "I have no religion. I'm a follower of Jesus."

With that, Dr. Jernigan, visiting from the conservative Christian college, walked quickly out of the building to have a smoke.

FOUR

THE WEEKEND DIDN'T CHANGE the news on the terrorists much, and by Monday morning, without new information to fuel the media machine, the story had slipped out of the national headlines. Locally, however, the story was radioactive. Anxiety had built up all weekend due to the constant discussion on talk shows of every variety. One piece of information was the most frightening, and it was the tidbit that was repeated the most: The pattern for al Qaeda was to be tenacious about any given target. Not to have others step in and finish an attack was seen as a personal failure and a failure before Allah. When the terrorists failed the first time to bring down the World Trade Center buildings in 1993, they tried again and were successful in 2001 and of course killed thousands. With the two Indonesian suspects still at large, many people's anxiety was sky-high.

Dr. Jernigan walked into the classroom two minutes late, whistling "Rainy Days and Mondays," a song by the Carpenters that the students were too young to recognize. He had on his trademark blue jacket with a stack of papers in one hand and an odd paper-wrapped package in the other. He set them down on the table in front.

He turned to the class and said, "Looks like we're missing some folks. Should we wait a few minutes to get started?"

All the students who would be in class had arrived, and in spite of the invitation for the students to bring friends, the class had about five fewer than on Friday.

Reagan said, "I got a place to park real easy today. I think people are staying away because of the terrorists."

"I don't blame them," he said, "the fear is palpable. But those of you bold enough to brave the mean streets of Laguna will be rewarded. Then he recited another saying:

> Assailed by fears, we discover truth
>
> And find the way to liberation. Thank you, fears.
>
> When sorrows invade the mind, we discover compassion
>
> And find lasting happiness. Thank you, sorrows.

Michael turned around and picked up the strange little package. It looked like it was from a previous century and was covered with wrinkled brown paper and some crisscrossing twine. He held it up to his face, looked at all sides, and then set it down again on the edge of the front table, hoping to draw attention to it. But then he said nothing about it.

"I suppose that at the beginning of the term you had a chance to go around the room and introduce yourselves, but it would be very helpful to me if we could do it again even though we're at the end of the semester," Michael suggested.

Without a break in her gum chewing, Charlene said, "No, I don't think we ever did that."

Michael had been a college teacher for years, so he could pretty quickly size up the dynamics of a classroom. Charlene was the spokesperson for the group. Reagan probably never sat near the front or spoke in her other classes on campus, but in this class, she drew strength from her friend Charlene.

"Well, fine then. That's an even better reason to do it now."

Michael sat on the table in front but on the opposite end from the package, which had its own dedicated space—a situation that added to its mystique. He listened intently as the students randomly volunteered to say a few things about themselves. Michael always did something like this on the first day of the semester, but never toward the end. The texture here was much different. Michael had mini dialogues with the first two students who volunteered, and his warmth and affirming tone put everyone at ease. Many of the students had already grown comfortable with each other, so they shared about themselves openly, including their own religious views.

Reagan Nguyen told the class that her family had come to the United States from Vietnam as part of the "boat people" refugee movement in 1975. Her grandmother, who lived with them, was a Buddhist, but her mother and father were Roman Catholics. Reagan's hair matched the bifurcated life she led. She had a razor-straight part down the middle of her head. The hair on the left was jet black, and the other side was a pastiche of pink colors. She was constantly being pulled by two cultures and two religions. But she was also being pulled by her family's expectations for achievement on one hand, and on the other, her desire to fit in with those her own age for whom school was not a top priority.

She candidly spoke about her own religious confusion and about her renewed interest in the Buddhism of her grandmother. When she finished, Michael responded,

> *Cái kiêp tu hành nang-dá deo*
> *Chi vì môt chút teo tèo teo*
> *Thuyên tu cung muôn vê Tây-trúc*
> *Trái gió cho nên phai lôn lèo.*

Reagan began to tear up and replied, "*Toi khong hieu.*"

Charlene had become pretty good friends with Reagan over the semester but had never heard her speak a different language. She didn't even know she could.

After a few more students, a woman named Virginia Renker introduced herself. Michael was looking forward to hearing her story because she was the only student who was more than twenty-five years old. Michael wondered if she was a few years older than him, but since so many women colored their hair and found ways to defy age, he was terrible at guessing. Certainly she was between fifty-five and sixty-five. He had never had a senior student in an undergraduate class at San Gabriel College. He'd had them in graduate classes, but that was a very different environment. He immediately thought she must be fairly adventurous to be on a campus full of late teens and very young twentysomethings. Of course, most of the students in the class didn't know her story either, so everyone's interest was high.

Virginia told the class that her husband had passed away suddenly a few years ago. She had lived in Laguna all her married life on Winchester Drive. (All the local students knew that meant she was probably very wealthy, and the jewelry she wore sometimes confirmed that.) The same year her husband died, her home was destroyed in the huge fire that consumed a dozen multimillion-dollar estates. Without hesitation she had rebuilt on the same lot. During this time of deep loss, she was seeing a counselor who encouraged her to begin attending meditation classes offered by a local spiritual teacher named Gyandev Rose. Her guru encouraged her to increase in all forms of knowledge, so she took that as a prompting to go back to college.

As she described her personal religious ideas and practices, she reminded Michael of a woman he had read about in recent sociology studies. Extensive surveys across the nation had identified an archetypal woman the researchers called "Sheila," who embodied the new American approach to religion. Sheila was the quintessential representative of the averages in all survey categories, and Virginia matched the Sheila profile point by point. Virginia said she believed in God but made a point of letting the class know she was not a religious fanatic. She couldn't remember the last time she went to church other than for weddings and funerals. Just like Sheila, Virginia was a "believer but not a belonger," and her faith was eclectic in that she felt free to incorporate anything she saw as attractive from any religious tradition.

Virginia wrapped up her comments by saying, "I think it's important just to love yourself and be kind to yourself and to others."

While Virginia was talking, Michael couldn't help thinking of Jesus, who had great compassion on the distressed and confused people of his day, saying they were like "sheep without a shepherd."

"Thank you, Virginia," Michael said. "I'm really happy that you and the others feel safe enough to share so much about your lives with us. This is a very rich time."

Darren Stevens' turn was next. He talked a little about his time at Stanford and the deal his dad made him to get him back on track. His fellow students knew from the quality of the questions he had asked Dr. Lightner in class that he had a lot more going on inside than the mindless surfer shtick. But apart from the questions in class, no one would have any clue that the surfer persona was not total. He was a great student for an early-morning class because if the waves were good, he would be up at five thirty and wide awake for the lecture. He was often in the hall before class, giving a report to his "brahs."

"Howzit, brah? It was weapons grade early, fully macking double-overhead corduroy to the horizon. But it got all buggery. So we ducked to the food hut and grabbed a breakfast burro and some sweet nectar. Latronic, dude."

Like some of the others, Darren felt free to open up about his religious views, and they seemed to parallel the rest of his intellectual life—an occasional remarkable insight or two and potential for brilliance, but severely lacking in the areas of hard work and focus that would get him there. He had a definite skeptical streak about religion in general, but it didn't go very deep. To support it, he normally just parroted some old and easily refutable chestnuts that he picked up from cynical high school teachers or from his dad and his dad's friends who were engineers.

"If I had to go with either religion or science, I'd totally go with science. I mean, you can really know stuff in science. You can repeat experiments and see things and measure things. You don't have to invoke invisible gods and spirits to figure things out," Darren said.

Michael was not challenging anybody's comments during this time of introduction, but he was tempted to address the false dichotomy Darren was drawing between religion and science. He was glad he didn't, though, because Darren continued.

"But like, I don't know, sometimes when I'm sitting on my board on the still water just beyond the breakers early in the morning...you know how the first sunlight climbs the mountain? Then the gray begins to glow red in some puffy clouds. And then purple, and then scarlet, and then gold as the sun keeps rising. You just want to shout up and down the coast, 'Carpe diem, Carpe diem!' I mean, it's hard not to believe in God sometimes."

On very rare occasions, Darren would find himself waxing eloquent like that while his friends were waxing their boards. Their response was usually something like, "Dude, what orifice did you pull that out of?"

Michael was surprised and couldn't hold back a broad smile. "You may have already learned this, but in the field of religious studies, the experience you describe is very important."

Charlene was shaking her head no. Guess they hadn't learned it, Michael concluded.

"Early last century, a famous scholar name Rudolf Otto from the University of Marburg in Germany called this a 'numinous' encounter. It's an experience that goes well beyond rational explanation. We've all had these. Sometimes we experience this during a religious service, in the middle of a concert, on a backpacking trip in the Sierras, or when seeing the birth of a child. Almost everyone who has an experience like this has a pretty strong personal sense that no branch of science is going to be able to offer an adequate explanation. Neurons, brain chemicals, atoms, molecules, quarks, energy, motion—the physical elements and laws of the universe—all of these things appear to be incapable of accounting for these common human events that Professor Otto called awe-filled, tremendous, unique, and seemingly wholly other."

With that, the introductions—sometimes turned therapy—completed their tour around the room, landing on the final volunteer, Charlene McKimmon. Michael already had a clue as to why this woman, who normally was so quick to speak in class, did not jump out in front. He had caught a glimpse of a frightened look on Charlene's face when Reagan fought back tears during her time. The same look appeared on her face when others in the class opened themselves up to vulnerable moments. He suspected that Charlene felt things very deeply and that the depth of her own emotion scared her witless.

Michael had seen this quite often at San Gabriel College in his new spiritual formation classes. Students with real intensity in their emotional makeup commonly built various walls and developed public personas that effectively plugged up the deep well of feelings. Of course, this was detrimental to their spiritual growth because these students were not in touch with who they really were, and they were uncomfortable with how God made them.

Michael's assumptions were right on the money, but they only told half the story of why Charlene was hoping this would all go away.

Given her outspokenness, the class was expecting more than the "name, rank, and serial number" kind of presentation she was giving. But things suddenly ramped up.

"As for my own religious tradition, I grew up in a Christian home and really didn't know much about other religions until this class," she said.

Michael had interacted briefly with almost every student in the class, and Charlene was no exception. "And with what Christian tradition does your family identify?"

"You mean like Baptist or Catholic or something?" she asked.

"Yes, that's what I mean," said Michael.

"I don't know if we have a denomination like that."

"Well, what church do you go to?" he asked.

"Shepherd Hills Community Church."

"Are you rel…" He paused. "Are you relatively happy there?"

"Yes, it's fine," she said nervously.

Michael was very glad he shifted gears mid-sentence. He was going to ask her if she was related to Lucas McKimmon, the pastor of Shepherd Hills, a church so big that people call it a gigachurch instead of a megachurch. It was one of the biggest churches in the country. Lucas McKimmon had been on the cover of *Time* magazine and had appeared several times on *Larry King Live*. Some reports said that Pastor McKimmon's family suffered because he was away from home so much.

Although he preached at his own church about half the Sundays a year, he was away taping his own daily television show and traveling to rallies and events around the world in between. Charlene felt the pain, but her much-younger brother felt it even more.

Michael knew Charlene's last name from the roll sheet that Willa e-mailed to him, but it never occurred to him that Lucas McKimmon's daughter would be attending the very secular Laguna City College—a school that was known primarily for having the largest and most radical gay and lesbian studies department on the West Coast. Charlene had a full-ride volleyball scholarship and a kill shot that could clear the deck on the other side of the court. Her father had only been to two games during her stellar high school career and had yet to see one of her college matches. Charlene had hopes of making the Olympic team in another year, trusting her father would show up at one of those matches.

Over the years, Michael taught hundreds of students like Charlene who were PKs—pastor's kids—many of whom faced some very special challenges. The pressure on these kids was enormous as whole congregations watched them as evidence of their pastor "truly living out the faith." After all, people expected godly men to have godly children. Michael thought this problem was the only real piece of evidence that favored the Roman Catholic insistence on a celibate clergy. Why put a kid through this? He couldn't imagine the multiplied challenges Charlene was facing from her position in that enormous fishbowl at Shepherd Hills.

As soon as Charlene finished her comments, the students began urging Professor Jernigan to tell his story.

For dramatic effect, he ignored their requests for a few moments, just staring at them with a nondescript expression and nodding almost imperceptibly. He then stood up from the corner of the table he was sitting on and took a rather long route to the other side of the table. He walked very slowly by the whiteboard. He picked up one of the marking pens, examined it closely, then put it back down. It looked like he was pondering what to do next, but he knew just where he was heading. He arrived at the other side of the table, an arm's length from the peculiar package he had carried in.

Michael said to the class, "You will certainly hear my story. Indeed, all that we will cover in the rest of our time this semester is impossible to separate from my story."

That said, he gently picked up the package, pulled on one of the strings, and untied the knot that held it closed.

FIVE

PROFESSOR JERNIGAN PULLED BACK the paper and delicately lifted out a small book about six inches high and five across. It had an ornate cover that once had vibrant colors but had faded significantly over the years. On the front was some unusual and beautifully adorned script. On the back cover was a line that wound its way from top to bottom like a snake crisscrossing the panel. At five points, strokes of paint interrupted the winding line, and at the top was a drawing that looked like a rising sun. The cover and pages were held together by ties that ran through two holes on the edge.

"I was one of those lucky Americans who were drafted to serve in the Army infantry in Vietnam. Because I had a pretty good ear for languages, the military used me a lot for sensitive missions when they didn't feel they could trust the local bilinguals." Michael was seriously downplaying his talents with languages. His knowledgeable colleagues considered him to be an outright genius, one of the best natural linguists they had ever encountered.

"I was a grunt at a firebase in 1970 when my lieutenant told me I had to go with a group of men who weren't wearing uniforms and that it was best if I didn't ask any questions because they wouldn't answer them anyway. We flew to an air base in Thailand—I wouldn't have known where we were, but I recognized the Thai language being spoken on the ground.

"The next day they had me change into civilian clothes. I remember thinking I looked like an idiot in the freshly pressed safari shirt and khaki pants—what was I supposed to be, a tourist? They might as well have given me an orange vest that said CIA across the front. We flew west by helicopter for about an hour and landed in a small clearing in a lush mountain region. I figured we were in western Cambodia. I was told to get my gear in hand and jump out the moment we touched ground. They said the Huey would be down for only a few seconds. Obviously, we weren't supposed to be there."

As he spoke to the class, Michael began playing with one of the buttons on his blue jacket—the fidgeting he did when he felt the need for nicotine.

"We hiked about seven clicks on a trail that obviously wasn't used much. Foliage had begun to recapture the route."

Darren Stevens interrupted, "What's a click?"

"Oh, sorry, it's a kilometer. The trail took us to the top of a ridge, where we could see an isolated valley in the distance with one central village surrounded by four others. I thought I was in Shangri-la. It was a beautiful day, no one was shooting at me, and a cool breeze was blowing at that elevation—an amazing respite from the oppressive heat.

"At that point the leader of the operation, Curt—he didn't give me a last name, and I'm not sure the first name was real—decided to tell me what my role was. He said I had two objectives: to learn to communicate with the villagers and to gain their confidence. He said, 'Ya gotta write it all down, and ya gotta teach us. We'll tell you more on a need-to-know basis.' I had a hundred questions to ask him and the other two men with us, but I took my lieutenant's advice and kept my mouth shut.

"We startled some farmers as we made our way into the central village. An elderly woman came out of a thatched dwelling and began talking at us in an excited way—we assumed she was angry or afraid. None of us had weapons showing, but we were carrying pistols, grenades, and claymore mines in our packs. After listening to the lady speak so loudly and clearly for a few moments, I knew my job was not going to be hard. She was obviously speaking a derivative of the main Khmer language I had already learned a lot about when I was on the Mekong Delta for two weeks—I met a lot of Cambodians there. But it was tricky because…"

Michael trailed off from his story and started to give some technical details about consonants, and vocal register, and the relationship to Pali and Sanskrit, which he had learned in his later studies. He caught himself and got back on track.

"So anyway, although the old woman was surprised and a little anxious, she was actually welcoming us and offering hospitality. Curt wanted us to go directly to the village leadership and introduce ourselves as best we could. I urged him to let me play with the village children for a few hours first. There's no better way to learn a spoken language quickly than to hear five- to eight-year-old children communicating with each other. Their vocabulary and sentence structure is very basic, they generally only use simple verb tenses, they don't include confusing humor or slang references, and they exaggerate their pronunciation, you know, the way their parents speak to them to teach them the language.

"The people of the village were very warm to us, and because of my time with the children, by that evening I was able to have awkward, preschool-level conversations with the adults. They began to focus their attention on me because I was the one who could communicate. They were ignoring my handlers, who were more than twice my age.

"These people called themselves the Cardamom after the name of the mountains surrounding them. Although I had just met these people, I felt that their lives seemed to have a unique texture. I assumed they were Buddhists along with almost all the rest of the Cambodian population, but they had a very odd five-sided temple as a center point and gathering place. The number five had great significance for the people, and their pentagonal temple was unlike anything I had seen before or have seen since.

"The next day we gained an audience with the elders of the village. The leaders of the people were three monks who had the job for life. When one died, the next oldest in the monastery would join the triumvirate. So all of them were old men—it was a kind of gerontocracy.

"I'd give anything to have a photo or video of that first meeting with them. I was twenty years old and looked about fifteen. I was rail thin and much taller than the elders, and quite a contrast with my red hair and freckles. My three handlers sat behind me as I attempted to speak and gesture my way through some basic greetings and pleasantries. I missed much of what they were saying, and I think the elders knew that. But I did understand that they were offering for us to stay with them as long as we'd like—a very trusting and generous invitation.

"The CIA guys wouldn't tell me how long we would be there, so it was hard for me to make a plan to learn the language and gain the people's confidence. I figured these guys had a mission to make allies in various villages for military advantages down the road—kind of like what happened with the Hmong people in Laos. But it didn't matter. They either didn't want to learn the language or weren't up to the task. I took copious notes and even developed an anglicized alphabet and vocalization scheme for them. It appeared more and more that they were just halfheartedly following orders and putting in their time. I couldn't blame them for relaxing. It was a rare opportunity in a war zone, and the peaceful mountain valley beat R&R in Saigon hands down. Of course they expected me to work and assigned me certain phrases to learn, but other than that they left me alone.

"I immersed myself in village life as much as the locals would allow and was understanding their language with some proficiency within days. They were still having a good deal of trouble understanding me, though, because my speaking was stilted and I still depended on my notes to recall certain words from their unusually large vocabulary.

"I had seen some examples of their writing on objects surrounding the temple and really wanted to learn to read it. It turned out, though, that very few people in the village were literate. Reading and writing were only formally taught by the elders to monks who might one day be elders. The elders acted as the scribes for the community.

"When we had been there about a week, we were invited to the monastery for an evening meal, and the elders were there. The man who seemed to me to be the chief and the oldest of the three leaders was delighted to be able to talk to me. I had no idea how old he actually was, but he was spry and energetic. He smiled constantly with a grin that was minus a tooth on the top and the matching one on the bottom, leaving a perfect vertical slot.

"His name was Map Nuth, and I told him my name was Michael, which he pronounced 'Micah' for the rest of my visit. It didn't take long to see why he was the leader. He was kind and disarming, but he was no fool. He gently prodded me for answers as to why we were there. Because of my handlers' secrecy toward me, I was able to tell him in all honesty that I was there to learn their language and to make new friends. He often glanced over at Curt and his men, indicating to me that he still harbored some moderate suspicions.

"I took the opportunity to ask him if he or another monk would teach me to read and write in Cardamom. He didn't answer me. He suddenly sprang to his feet—I meant it when I said he was spry—and quickly shuffled away, barking a word that either meant "go" or "wait." My heart skipped a beat, and I thought, *Uh-oh, I probably just seriously crossed some line.* I wasn't exactly a trained diplomat. Curt saw Master Nuth move quickly out of the room gesturing and shouting and saw the startled expression on my face. Curt was alarmed and reached behind his back to his waistline, where I suspected he had a weapon.

"The barking faded out as Master Nuth left the room. After a moment or two of silence, the barking built up steam again as he headed back toward us. He emerged holding something bundled in a dried banana leaf. Curt's eyes were riveted on the old man, and his hand was still positioned at the small of his back. Master Nuth sat down next to me, pulled back the wrapping, and showed me this very palm-leaf manuscript."

Michael held it up to show the class. He didn't like to touch it with his bare hands very often, but he made an exception. He walked slowly around the room so everyone could have a close look and then set it back on its acid-free protective wrapping. He continued the story.

"Curt immediately let down his guard and went back to eating the fruit that was in front of him. Master Nuth put on some reading glasses, which indicated to me that the villagers had at least some trading contact with more civilized towns. He was very excited about showing me the book and was speaking a little more quickly than I could handle. His face was in the book, so I couldn't see his lips move, which certainly didn't help me. All I could pick up was that the book was called *The Five* somethings and that he would allow me to study it with the initiates in the *Sangha,* the community of monks. At first I was afraid he thought I wanted to become an initiate, but it turned out he just liked me and wanted to serve. But more importantly, Master Nuth wanted me to learn the lessons from this book, which had transformed the Cardamom people generations ago."

Michael sat back down on the teacher's table in front and picked up the book one more time. He said, "This really is a remarkable book. Probably the best translation of the title is *Five Sacred Crossings,* but the villagers referred to it simply as *The Five Crossings.* The text is fairly brief, but as you can see, the calligraphy is magnificent, and each page is illuminated with drawings and figures similar to a medieval biblical text. It's certainly a work of art. But the villagers would be offended if we made too much of the visual beauty. In that respect, it reminds me of a Tibetan sand mandala. Have you ever seen one of those? Exquisite paintings made completely out of sand that exist only for a few days. Then they are destroyed in a single motion to illustrate the Buddhist view of the impermanent nature of all things. The Cardamom have a similar belief—that one should move quickly beyond the visual beauty of the book and into the transcendent message of spiritual balance."

The students were deeply interested in the message of the book, but the class time was almost over.

"Dr. Jernigan," said Reagan, "you can't leave us hanging about what happened in the village. We only have a few more minutes."

"Oh yeah. Thanks for watching the clock. Well, I studied with the monks for weeks and got a good handle on their written language. But more importantly, I got a chance to see them live out their teachings.

"I'll never forget when Map Nuth asked me to accompany him to visit a tribe of people in another valley. It was just me, Master Nuth, and one other young initiate, probably around my age. Both of us had trouble keeping up with the elder over the mountains. The CIA guys wanted me to make a map, but I didn't. When we arrived, we went to a central gathering place in the village, sort of like a town square. They had set up some low tables, prepared lots of food, and positioned sitting mats around the tables. It was a great scene—it looked to me like Master Nuth was quite a visiting dignitary, and the whole village had prepared a celebration for his visit. One set of tables was decorated with the finest flowers and looked like it was the place of honor. As I was taking it all in, they began to call people to sit. I turned around to look for Master Nuth, and there he was, sitting on a mat at the other end of the square—at what looked like the children's table. The chiefs of the town all walked down to him and attempted to talk him into sitting at the fine table with the village leaders. I couldn't make out what they were saying, but it was an energetic conversation with lots of gesturing. Finally, they lifted Map Nuth to his feet, and he relented and followed them to the head table.

"On the way back to his village, Master Nuth walked more slowly so he could talk with us about the incident. He said that it was never wise to immediately take a seat in a place of honor. What would happen if someone of greater stature came to the table? You would be humiliated as you had to move to a lower position. But if you sit on the lowliest mat and your hosts ask you to take a seat at the table of the elders, it is a double honor to you and to your family.

"Living with the Cardamom and studying at the *Sangha* was an amazing personal spiritual journey. It may be the greatest irony on the planet that a grubby CIA mission led me into one of the most valuable spiritual lessons I could ever imagine.

"I was bowled over by Map Nuth and the other senior leaders in the religious community. Their example of compassion and wisdom was unlike anything I had seen before or have seen since. Buddhism is my area of specialty, and I haven't seen or heard of anything that compares to this group. Looking back, I can't classify them as Buddhists. All I can say about them is what they said about themselves: 'We are the people of *The Five Crossings.*'

"My time with them ended quickly and without warning. One night, Curt got a radio call, and we hiked out to meet a helicopter before dawn. No goodbyes or words of thanks to those remarkable, generous people. I was with my old unit in Nam going out on ambush the very next night, terrified beyond belief.

"Let me close with a postscript that I think is more touching than anything else I've said so far. I have not been back to visit the Cardamom since my tour in Vietnam. I longed to go to them when I was doing research in Thailand in 1982, but of course this time I didn't have a CIA helicopter at my disposal, and the journey was too far and too dangerous for an American tourist. But in Bangkok, I bumped into a missionary couple who had reports about the Cardamom people.

"As you probably know, from 1976 to 1979 the murderous Khmer Rouge regime was in power under Pol Pot in Cambodia, and they wiped out millions of intellectuals and whole villages in their infamous killing fields. Religious leaders were especially targeted for extermination. The missionaries filled me in on what happened with the Cardamom. It seems that during this terrible time in Cambodian history, the Khmer Rouge execution squads marched up to the mountain valley of the Cardamom to slaughter the religious community, and they were met on the trail by none other than Master Map Nuth, standing alone.

"As the people of the village tell it, Map Nuth was taken by the Khmer Rouge soldiers, who then turned away from the village. Map Nuth was never seen again. When the Cardamom tell the story, they say that Map Nuth gave himself up for his dear ones—the village people—and for something called the 'Fifth Crossing.'

"Several years later, when Pol Pot had been toppled and the country was more stable, a group of Christian missionaries made plans to visit the Cardamom. These missionaries had learned the language from travelers who traded with the mountain people, and they had prepared a translation of the Gospel of John to bring to the Cardamom.

"It is certainly a rare occurrence in the annals of religious history, but when the missionaries arrived and began to teach about Jesus and read to them the Gospel of John, the elders and the entire village embraced the message almost without question. As the missionaries report it, the people said, 'We have been awaiting this time of visitation. We knew about this man of deliverance.' It turned out that *The Five Crossings* had prepared them for the saving message about Jesus.

"Of course, I still long to go back to these people and hear their amazing story."

Michael had gone seven minutes past the official end of class, and no one wanted it to end there. They had all been transported a world away from the fear and anxiety that terrorists had caused to wash over Laguna City College.

SIX

A MASSIVE MANHUNT WAS in progress for the two terror suspects, but no photos had yet been released to the public. This was simply because no photos had yet been found. Finally, on Monday afternoon, some grainy pictures of one of the young men were discovered on an LCC student's camera phone. They were enhanced and then displayed widely in newspapers and on television all day on Tuesday. New leads began popping up. After seeing the photos, the manager of a self-storage facility on the other side of town called the authorities to report that he might have rented a ground-floor unit to one of the Indonesian students.

Authorities evacuated several blocks surrounding the facility even before the bomb squad arrived with explosive-sniffing dogs. The dogs gave a positive reading on one of the units, but it wasn't the one the suspect had rented. The technicians drilled a small hole in the top of the unit and used a fiber-optic camera to view the contents while the FBI picked up the renter at work—a dentist who was in the middle of performing a root canal. The man was questioned and admitted to a less-than-federal crime: storing a box of illegal fireworks.

When the bomb squad officers went back to their truck for a break, the field commander immediately noticed that their radiation badges had changed color. The dosimeters were showing a glow curve that was off the charts. Some serious radiation was coming from somewhere in the storage yard—presumably from the unit rented by the Indonesian suspect.

An evacuation order went out on Tuesday afternoon for a one-mile radius from the storage units. Almost a quarter of the city was affected. The antiterrorism experts knew, though, that if they were actually dealing with a nuclear device or some kind of radioactive dirty bomb, the evacuation was just window dressing.

⋅✦⟨✛⟩✦⋅

"It's amazing how we go about our routines even though all hell is breaking loose around us," Michael said to the class as they settled into their seats. He had just walked in himself whistling "Top of the World" by the Carpenters.

"I knew guys in Vietnam who would brush their teeth or wash their socks at the appointed time even if it was in the middle of a rocket attack. Their routine kept them sane. Looks like the routine of coming to class wasn't strong enough for everyone though. What, we have two more missing, Barnes and Sosa? Maybe they're just sick, huh? Dr. Lightner isn't going to be happy with me if I lose the whole group before the final."

Michael was making small talk to give another minute for stragglers and to try to put people at ease. But he was worried himself. LCC was less than a quarter mile outside the evacuation zone.

"Dr. Jernigan, routine isn't doin' it for me. I'm ditchin' calculus and history today. I'm only here cuz I want to hear more about Map Nuth and *The Five Crossings*," admitted Darren. "My house got tagged for evacuation, so I'm campin' at the Point, where it's safe. And the Mexican hurricane happens to be causing epic surf right now."

"So you're going down to surf the Point? Right in front of San Baldera Nuclear Power Plant? With two terrorist bombers on the loose? And you don't think routine is a strong drive for you?" Michael said, trying to help alert Darren to the danger involved.

"Dude, the way I got it figured, the area around the nuclear plant is the safest place in the country right now. They probably quintupled their security measures."

"Hey, you're right. Good point…about the Point," Michael responded. He learned his lesson this time. Darren's surfing persona was *not* an indicator of low IQ or excessive pot smoking.

Virginia Renker had moved up a row from her usual seat in class because she was so enthralled by the story of the Cardamom people. "They evacuated my area too," she said, "so I'm only here today to find out more about *The Five Crossings*. My spiritual advisor, Gyandev Rose, has never heard of this, so he's curious too."

"Well, feel free to invite him to class anytime," said Michael.

Michael pulled some cloth gloves out of his jacket pocket and slipped them on his hands. "I really should have worn these on Monday," he said. He then unwrapped the book and picked it up. "A friend of mine is a professional archivist and said I need to be extra careful handling a palm-leaf manuscript. Master Nuth never told me how old it was. In fact, he made it sound like it was a brand-new copy even though it looked worn and old to me thirty years ago. The archivist told me that this is probably 100 to 150 years old. Each of the monks in training had his own copy, and each copy had been penned by an elder of the Cardamom. Map Nuth gave this to me to keep in such a nonchalant way that at first I thought they must have a crate of them in a closet somewhere. But it's a very rare and precious volume."

Reagan Nguyen was in the front row, and her eyes were locked on the cover. "Could you tell us about the artwork on the back?" she asked. "What's the snake supposed to symbolize?"

Michael brought the book closer for her to see. "It's not a snake; it's a river winding through the countryside. It's small and faded, so you have to look closely, but the ink drawing at the bottom represents a dark, ominous jungle where confusion and danger reign."

Virginia was sitting forward with her reading glasses on, waiting for him to bring it closer to her.

"The large rising sun at the top is easy to see, but if you look closely you can see that the sun is rising over the mountains," he continued. "This is where peace, refuge, safety, harmony, and balance abound. The markings at five spots along the river are points of crossing. Again, if you look closely, these are bridges of sorts. The image is faded and smudged, but if you look at this one in the middle you can see the detail—it's a rope bridge. The one below it is not a bridge at all, but rather a set of stepping-stones. This isn't meant to be a map to guide people through the terrain—although maybe it could in a rudimentary way. Rather, it represents that the land itself is telling a story. The created order has signposts that everyone should heed."

Michael was a scholar and normally used a methodical setup to make his points and cover all his bases when dealing with an ancient text. His plan was to spend the whole class time talking about language synthesis and the obvious confluence of worldviews from South Asia and the Indian subcontinent in this unusual work. He had spent several minutes going down this path when Charlene raised her hand and halted his momentum.

"Dr. Jernigan, I know this is really important stuff, but speaking as one who's risking her life to be here this morning, do you think we can talk a bit less about the book and maybe jump into what's in it? I'm very anxious to know what the big secret is about *The Five Crossings*."

Virginia wanted to nod in agreement but didn't want to be associated with Charlene's overly dramatic lead-in. Michael apologized to the class, thanked Charlene, and immediately shifted gears. No one complained—Charlene had spoken for the entire class. Michael was normally pretty sensitive to these class dynamics but missed this one completely.

"Map Nuth and the other elders emphasized two things over and over again to their students about *The Five Crossings*. First, the book itself is not holy or sacred, but is a guide to find that which is holy, sacred, eternal, or transcendent. Showing its debt to Buddhist thought, the text is supposed to disappear for an individual as the spiritual journey moves forward and, as they like to say, 'the sun rises higher over the mountains.' Second, the book is a community text. That is, it is meant to be discussed, wrestled with, and argued about. The Cardamom believe that engaging the text and its teachers is a spiritually enriching experience so long as it's done thoughtfully and with respect. Even though only the monks were fully literate, the lay people often sat through readings of *The Five Crossings* and were also encouraged to ask questions and discuss it thoroughly. I think their approach came from generations of wisdom and experience, so I think we should approach it the same way."

"But who wrote the book? I mean, where did they get it?" asked Charlene.

Michael felt mildly perturbed that she would ask because that was one of the important background points he was going to cover in his introductory lecture, which she interrupted.

"Well, very briefly, the Cardamom teach that the five basic points of wisdom were written by a great sage of the high country long ago. I don't know anyone who can give a precise date for that. Maybe as we get to know more about these people, scholars can answer that question, but the Cardamom simply say it was from 'generations past.' This sage was a leader of the people and had a vivid dream. In this dream he was trying to get home from a dark place, like the jungle on the book cover. And to make this journey he had to manage five difficult crossings of the river, which was swollen by monsoonal rains.

"At each crossing, he dreamed he was given wise counsel by otherworldly messengers, and each time the message was a spiritual raft that carried him safely across. The Fifth Crossing, though, was unique. In the dream, the messenger at this last crossing was more glorious than all the others combined, and the message was so powerful that it supernaturally transported the sage across the most dangerous crossing of all. And then the messenger had strength left to usher in the dawn as the sage made it safely back to his people."

Virginia was eating this up. She was trying to write everything down. Darren, on the other hand, was wondering if he should have left for the beach already. He didn't look impressed as he raised his hand.

"This is beginning to sound an awful lot like the other myths and religions we've gone over this semester—an angel visiting Muhammad in Islam, Krishna's revelation to Arjuna in Hinduism, the Kachina doll in the Hopi religion. Dr. J., you don't seem like the typical religious type. What drew you into all this? It's all so mystical sounding."

"Thus far, I'd have to agree with you, Darren. But I think you'll be pleasantly surprised at the different texture of religious thinking presented by the Cardamom teachers. Their entire project is to engage the spirit *and* the mind in a perfect balance. Although they are an isolated people and may never have read Plato, Shakespeare, or Lao Tzu, they have a simple but profound wisdom tradition of their own that I'd put up against any through history.

"It's time we read some of their material together. Let's start with the central aphorisms of *The Five Crossings*."

Michael handed each student a photocopy of a sheet of paper he had prepared with exotic Cardamom script and his English translation. They read them out loud together.

The First Crossing
Spiritual knowledge springs from within and from without
Where one is absent the other is void

The Second Crossing
Only one hope remains for liberation
The greatest of gifts must be free

The Third Crossing
Everyone must paint a landscape
Eternal wisdom is with those whose eye is true

The Fourth Crossing
Wisdom does not live in two rooms
Knowledge divided invites shadows in the soul

The Fifth Crossing
The one who transcends boundaries
Is he who brings deliverance

Darren still looked skeptical, and Charlene seemed to have joined him in that frame of mind after the reading. He said, "I'll be honest with you, Dr. J., that didn't help very much. Why does all religion have to be so mystical and ambiguous?"

"I'll tell you what," said Michael. "After today we have five class meetings left. During each one we will use one of the core aphorisms in our teaching and discussion the same way the monks in the village did. I'll play the role of Master Nuth, God rest his soul. I'll teach and prod and ask questions about spiritual issues. Your job is to respond from your thinking and experience in a quest for real spiritual balance."

The class seemed up for that—Virginia and Reagan especially so.

"But one last thing. Make sure you empty your cups first. The Cardamom offer an exciting new tea, but if your cup is already full, you won't be able to appreciate it."

Michael paused for a moment and said again, "Empty your cup. I'll see you Friday morning."

SEVEN

THE EVACUATION ORDER FOR half of the population in Laguna had been lifted. Federal agents and radiation experts had worked around the clock to identify the contents of the storage unit. The type of radiation being emitted eliminated the possibility of a nuclear device. Bomb-detecting dogs gave no positive hits for any of the chemicals used in explosives, so a radioactive dirty bomb sitting inside the unit was unlikely. Video cameras threaded through holes in the storage unit did not detect any imminent danger or booby traps.

The radiation signatures coming from inside did not put any of the investigators at ease, though. A very hot cache of cesium-137 was sitting somewhere inside—the radionuclide of choice for anyone wishing to make a dirty bomb. Because of the attention drawn by the evacuation, everyone in town now knew what a dirty bomb was. It wasn't a powerful explosive that could wipe out a whole city with its blast. A dirty bomb was a conventional explosive—like TNT, an artillery shell, or an ammonium nitrate–fuel oil mixture—to which was strapped dangerous radioactive material for wide dispersal. Experts on TV were saying that if a bomb like that went off, the poisonous radiation could make a city like Laguna uninhabitable for fifty or sixty years.

After setting up very tight radiation protections, the authorities opened the storage unit and found a lead container that had not been resealed properly. The container was mostly empty, and the entire unit was contaminated by the remaining powder. The two Indonesian suspects evidently had access to all the materials necessary for a catastrophic attack. Whether the plot had been discovered in time, no one knew.

✦❖✦

Michael was a couple of minutes late to class because he was out of cigarettes and had to stop on the way, buy some, and smoke one before class. He didn't tell the students why he was walking in late, but he had the sense of well-being that caffeine and nicotine can bring in the morning and was whistling "Yesterday Once More" by the Carpenters.

"Dr. J., you gotta get a new CD or shuffle the list on your iPod. You're always whistling the most deluxe geezer music. That stuff's not even fit for elevators at my grandma's apartment building," Darren said.

Michael smiled and laughed and shook his head all at the same time. He and Darren had talked for fifteen minutes after class last time and really hit it off. Then Michael noticed that only a few of the seats in the room were empty. All the students on the roll sheet were there, and several students had brought friends in—including Virginia, who brought a tanned man with a well-coiffed head of gray hair that covered his ears in a 1970s style. His shirt was unbuttoned just enough to reveal a gold chain and a little bit of gray hair on his chest.

"Welcome, everyone. Glad to see such a full house. I'm assuming everyone's feeling a little better about life now that the evacuation order's been lifted," Michael said.

"Dr. Jernigan, I brought a guest today. I'd like to introduce my friend Gyandev Rose," Virginia said.

Michael noticed their desk chairs were a bit closer together than most and suspected there was something a little more than a friendship in the works.

"It's a pleasure to meet you. Gyandev? Are you named after Sant Gyaneshwar, the thirteenth-century Indian poet and commentator on the Gita?" asked Michael.

Gyandev, who looked as if he could have been born and raised in Malibu, simply answered no. He offered no explanation for the classical Indian name. Receiving such a terse reply, Michael decided not to ask any follow-up questions. A few other students introduced their guests, and Michael began the session.

"As I said on Wednesday, we'll follow the tradition of the Cardamom in exploring *The Five Crossings.* They followed a fivefold pattern when learning as a community. First they spent some significant time meditating on the message of the aphorism. Sometimes they spent a whole day just on the meditative portion of the exercise. Of course, we'll have to shorten the process significantly. Second, they 'opened the door to the winds,' as they called it. The initiates—that will be you—were free to share their initial insights and reflections in a free-ranging discussion. Third, the revered teacher—that will be me in this case—" Michael said with a grin, "gave the 'elder's discourse' on the Crossing, sharing his wisdom or the wisdom of the sages of the past. The fourth and fifth steps in the process were the first two in reverse. The initiates again had open discussion and then read the aphorism together one last time to close."

Reagan raised her hand and said, "But we know almost nothing about their culture. How are we supposed to interact with their ideas?"

"Oh right, right. Glad you asked that. Very important point," said Michael. "According to Master Nuth, the Five Crossings are supposed to be universal principles, necessary steps for anyone to achieve a true balance in mind and spirit. Therefore, we don't need to draw on examples or teachings or cultural artifacts from the mountain regions of Cambodia alone. If these principles hold, they'll stand up to our questions, our life experiences, and our probing from our own time and place.

"Have you emptied your cups? Then let's start. Take a few minutes to think carefully about the meaning of this."

Michael turned to the whiteboard and wrote these lines:

The First Crossing
Spiritual knowledge springs from within and from without
Where one is absent the other is void

The class sat silently staring at the aphorism. After about thirty seconds, most were looking around and wondering what to do next. They were waiting for Michael to take the lead. Michael had pulled up a chair and sat with the class, reading the whiteboard.

After one minute, the silence was very uncomfortable. American students rarely had moments of quiet reflection. Constant, intense background noise filled almost every waking moment of their lives. Michael would have liked to give it much longer, but after five very long minutes he turned his chair around and said, "Let us open the door to the winds."

Charlene could not have broken the spirit of the moment more thoroughly. "Is this legal? I mean, aren't we reading their holy book and doing their religion? We can learn about religion, but isn't it out of bounds to practice religion in a class like this?"

She was looking at Michael to answer, but he didn't flinch. He sat still and silent. After a few more moments of silence, Reagan spoke up. "Charlene, that was a strange thing to ask. It doesn't look to me like anybody is being asked to believe anything, just to understand the way another group approaches religion, to walk in their moccasins, so to speak. That's what we've been doing one way or another all semester. What do you think of the aphorism?"

"I don't know what it's supposed to be saying, it's so vague," Charlene replied.

Darren, dropping all surf jargon and sounding a bit like his dad, the aerospace engineer, said, "It does sound a lot like the kind of religious language we've heard from the other traditions. But I suppose we can break it down to a few basic ideas. I don't know what 'spiritual knowledge' is, but whatever it is, it looks like it can come from two places: from inside the person and from outside the person. I'm assuming knowledge from the inside means a feeling I have about something or a creative idea that only I know. And I'm guessing that knowledge from outside means knowing things that are external to us through sense perception—things that we can all know. That all seems pretty obvious, but that's all I'm getting from it."

Virginia said, "I practiced Zen for a while before I started studying with Gyandev, and my Zen teacher always emphasized that no real knowledge comes from the outside. Real knowledge, spiritual insight, enlightenment, derives only from the inside."

Gyandev nodded in agreement with that.

"See, I don't know what that means," said Darren. "Does that mean I can't know that there's a whiteboard on the wall because it's knowledge that seems to be coming to me from the outside? I really do think we can know that there's a whiteboard right there, and it gives me a headache when people begin to question that."

Reagan said, "But isn't it different when we're talking about religious things? I can see the whiteboard, and I think I can claim to know that. But is God here right now? I can't see him if he is. It's really funny at my house when my Catholic parents sometimes argue with my Buddhist grandmother. My parents claim that we all have souls while my grandmother says that we have no souls. Doesn't that sound silly? They are arguing over something no one can see. No one can know one way or the other if the soul exists, but they argue over it."

Up to this point Charlene seemed either bored or annoyed with the discussion, but she perked up over Reagan's comment. "I think we can know that we have a soul."

"How do we know that?" asked Reagan.

"Well, the fact that we're moving around and talking and thinking means we have a soul, and besides, the Bible says we have a soul," said Charlene.

Darren said, "I went to the emergency room a couple of months ago because my parents thought I might have pneumonia. So I go in and see this sophisticated medical equipment, and not a single piece of it was designed to tell me if I have a soul or how my soul is doing. They could do all kinds of things to tell me about the state of my body but nothing about my soul. They even took a chest X-ray. They looked right inside me and still didn't see a soul."

"That doesn't prove you don't have a soul," Charlene countered.

"Yeah, but it does show that the soul is something you either believe in or you don't. It certainly isn't something we can know in the same way that we know the whiteboard is on the wall," said Darren.

"It's definitely all about faith," Reagan asserted. "That's the one thing my parents and grandmother agree on. That's why they still get along in spite of their different religious views. They know religious things are personal, and faith is how you know them. Believing that the Bible teaches that humans have souls is the same thing. You either believe the Bible or you don't."

The entire class got into the discussion, and it continued for some time. Except for a few holdouts, the students in the class agreed that personal faith was the only common denominator in the whole business of religion.

Charlene then said something that again broke the spirit of the moment, but this time in a productive way. "So everyone seems to agree that faith is the key to understanding spiritual knowledge. But I'm trying to relate this to the First Crossing. Is faith a kind of spiritual knowledge that we discover inside us, or is it the kind of knowledge we get from the outside—like seeing the whiteboard?"

Almost everyone agreed that faith was all about inner beliefs, feelings, and personal spiritual knowledge.

Charlene said, "Then none of us is really agreeing with the Cardamom aphorism because it says that spiritual knowledge comes from outside too, and if it doesn't, the whole thing, according to them, is bogus or void or whatever."

Michael was extremely pleased at the level of discussion that was going on, but he wasn't surprised. He had seen the Five Crossings work their magic in the past. The Cardamom had developed an extremely effective method of community learning. But now it was his turn to give the elder's discourse. Sometimes the elders told stories that illustrated important points; sometimes they presented arguments that supported a favored position. But either way, the goal of the elder's discourse was to help the entire community move to a new level of understanding and on to the next Crossing.

Michael stood up and spoke the transition phrase he had

67

Five Sacred Crossings

learned from Master Nuth: "The wind is now howling, and it is time to shut the door."

The students looked at him a little puzzled.

"It is time for the elder's discourse, or as Darren might say, the geezer speech. Let me illustrate an important truth about the First Crossing with a story from my own Christian tradition that I think will provide some wisdom on the issues we've been discussing. It begins with a story that comes from the New Testament in the Gospel of Mark.

"Mark tells the story of a remarkable visit Jesus made to the city of Capernaum, a city on the north shore of the Sea of Galilee about sixty miles north of Jerusalem. Jesus had already gained a reputation as a spellbinding itinerant preacher and healer. The text says Jesus was teaching in a local home and that the place was filled to overflowing with a crowd of curious people and new followers—not surprising at all in a day when cable TV, multiplex theaters, and video games were nonexistent. This was certainly the hottest ticket in town, both high-level entertainment as well as religious nurturing.

"The story takes a very touching turn when some men in town who had heard about Jesus' ability to heal run out to fetch a friend of theirs. Their friend was paralyzed—a tragic situation that could be a lifetime sentence to beg for a living in those times. The four men loaded their friend onto a mat and carried him to the home where Jesus was teaching. Unfortunately, the crowd was so big, they weren't able to get their friend anywhere near Jesus. But they were a resourceful and energetic bunch, so they found a way to climb up on the roof of the dwelling with their paralytic friend.

"Now imagine the scene inside the home as the four men above start to dig through the earthen roof. Suddenly dirt clods and dust begin to fall right in the middle of Jesus' message. Then a beam of sunlight leaps down into the room as the men break through the roof. I'm sure the commotion punctuated in dramatic fashion whatever Jesus was saying at the time. You can just picture the scene. More debris falls down as the hole in the roof gets bigger, and the beam of light turns into a broad spotlight. Then a head pops through the hole, looks around the room, and pops back up.

The hole gets a little bigger, and dust fills the air. The light pouring in through the thick atmosphere gives the whole room an ethereal feel.

"The people who got there early were elated. Even though by this time they were covered in dust, they were thrilled to be there. Nothing like this ever happened in this small town. Then it got even better. A young man on a mat being lowered by ropes begins to descend toward Jesus.

"He lands near Jesus' feet, and people around the room begin to recognize that this man is the one who begs for food and money at the entrance to the town. All eyes then move from the young man to Jesus. What will he do? The crowd leans forward breathlessly to hear the new teacher's response.

"Keeping in line with the strange tenor of the moment, the first thing out of Jesus' mouth is something completely unexpected. He looks at the young man on the ground in front of him and says, 'Son, your sins are forgiven.'

"The people in the house stare at Jesus in silence, a bit puzzled, and then look at each other as if to ask, 'What did he say? Is that kosher?' Mark's account says that some 'teachers of the law' were in the room listening to Jesus, and the text is clear that they didn't say anything but rather were thinking to themselves, *Why does this fellow talk like that? He's blaspheming! Who can forgive sins but God alone?*

"This can only be characterized as a dramatic situation on steroids. Here they are, in a land and a time where people are very unsettled with their government, both political and religious. You've got a crowd flowing out into the street with huge expectations about Jesus—many with the hope that he'll be their political deliverer. You've got a paralyzed man descending from a hole in the roof and dust in the air that hasn't yet settled. You have his friends peering in through the hole they dug. You have Jesus saying something that is by any measure outlandish for a mere mortal to say. And you have a conflict brewing with respected experts over Jesus' radical declaration. So in light of all this, what does Jesus do?

"The text says that Jesus knew immediately in his spirit what the teachers of the law were thinking. Not a bad gift to have in this situation. It doesn't say how he manifested this gift—if it was a supernatural kind of mind reading or simply a keen ability to accurately interpret the Grinch-like looks on their faces in the back of the room. Either way, his next move was to announce their thoughts out loud. 'Why are you thinking these things?' Jesus asked.

"Jesus put the teachers of the law, the learned skeptics of his day, in a difficult position. They had two choices about Jesus' identity. He was either a blasphemer who was a pretender to the unique divine privilege to forgive sins, or he was indeed God in human flesh dwelling among them. Probably nobody in the room, even Jesus' closest companions, were ready at this point to say he was the latter—but they were about to get some unmistakable clues right then and there.

"When Jesus declared that the paralyzed man's sins were forgiven, he was engaging in an activity that was invisible, spiritual, and untestable. In terms of the First Crossing, this would be an action that we would have to put into the 'spiritual knowledge from within' category. After all, if Jesus was really forgiving that man's sins, how would anyone in the room know that it was really happening? It was a true circumstance in which you either believe it or you don't.

"Therefore, most people who heard Jesus say this probably weren't moved very deeply by it. If you think about it, anybody could walk into a room like that and claim to forgive sins. I could imagine a huge religious spectacle in which I walk into this classroom with flowing robes, white beard, sandals, and a long staff and say 'Lo, my children. Your sins, they are forgiven.' Now you might think that's a wonderful sentiment, a very thoughtful thing for me to say. But how would you know if it really happened if it is by its very nature an invisible, spiritual activity?

"There is no way for the audience to *know* that sins were really being forgiven except for Jesus' words. You could claim you were forgiving sins all day, and no one could disprove your claim. Religious people make these kinds of claims all the time and then expect their followers to embrace the claims with a kind of blind faith.

"But then Jesus parts company with other religious people who make untestable spiritual claims. At the height of the dramatic moment, with the dust still swirling in the air, Jesus did something that sets him apart and that I believe captures the spirit of the First Crossing. Listen carefully to this." Michael read directly from the Gospel of Mark:

> "But that you may know that the Son of Man
> [that is, Jesus] has the authority on earth to forgive
> sins...." He said to the paralytic, "I tell you, get up, take
> your mat and go home." He got up, took his
> mat and walked out in full view of them all. This
> amazed everyone and they praised God, saying,
> "We have never seen anything like this!"

"Jesus wanted the people he was teaching to have *knowledge*," Michael continued, "not just blind faith or belief. His goal was not just to give them some mystical insights or an ineffable awareness. He wanted them to *know* something very important, so he linked the invisible act of forgiving sins with the very tangible act of commanding a paralyzed man to rise and walk miraculously. In terms of the First Crossing, the spiritual knowledge springing from within (the paralytic's sense or hope that his sins were forgiven) was confirmed by knowledge from without—a tangible public demonstration that authenticated the inner spiritual knowledge.

"I think this is the essence of what the Cardamom are after in the First Crossing. True spiritual balance is impossible if all of our religious views are derived from untestable, subjective, inner claims to knowledge. We must have some grounding in what can be known in an objective, public way.

"A former teacher of mine used to tell a story about a French statesman by the name of Louis-Marie de La Révellière-Lépeaux, who lived during the French Revolution. Like many in Paris during this time, La Révellière had a deep loathing of Christianity and the church. He ended up supporting a new kind of religious philosophy called theophilanthropism, which sought to elevate civic duty and public morality and treated only as useful sentiments the ideas that God exists and humans have immortal souls.

"As La Révellière was making a presentation of his new system of belief in hopes that it might officially replace Christianity in France, another French statesman who was known for his wit, Charles-Maurice de Talleyrand-Périgard, listened patiently to his case. When La Révellière was finished, Talleyrand responded to him, 'Well, this is all very interesting; you have made a very good presentation. But it seems to me that Jesus, in order to found his religion, died on a cross and came back to life on the third day. Perhaps you could at least do that much.'

"I think the Cardamom would have enjoyed Talleyrand because like them he was not interested in basing his most important life commitments on other people's inner religious whims. He also knew the importance of looking for outside confirmation. 'Where one is absent, the other is void.'"

Michael paused for a moment, and Charlene took that as the end of the elder's discourse. Fortunately she was right. "Do *we* get to talk again?" she asked.

Michael said, "Yes, it's time for the second discussion, but according to tradition, I'm supposed to say, 'The voice from the ages has spoken.' There, I've said it. So please, everyone, share your comments."

Gyandev was leaning over and whispering to Virginia.

"I think I see what you're saying," said Darren. "But I don't see how telling a religious story about Jesus is going to help us understand another religious story about the Five Crossings. Isn't that just religion feeding on religion? It doesn't seem like it can go anywhere."

"What do you mean by religion?" asked Charlene. "When you use that word, you're making it sound like the story never really happened, like it's some kind of fairy tale."

Darren replied, "No, I just mean that it's another example of the kind of thing you either believe or you don't. Like most of us agreed earlier, it's really all about faith. If you think it's true, awesome. I'm sure it can be really helpful to people."

"I'm getting confused. I thought Dr. Jernigan told that story about the healing of the paralyzed man because he believed it really happened, not because it was just a religious story," said Charlene.

Michael showed great restraint not jumping in to the discussion. Gyandev continued to whisper to Virginia.

"Oh, I don't think so," said Darren looking at Michael as if to prompt him to say something. "He certainly studied enough religion to know that all of these traditions have their stories—and for the most part they are only meant to convey spiritual truths."

"But what if it really happened?" Charlene asked. "What if Jesus really did miraculously heal that paralyzed man? What if Jesus really did come back from the dead on the first Easter Sunday?"

Darren paused for a moment, looking as if he was calculating the value of various responses. The question caught him off guard. His hesitation demonstrated the power a tightly held worldview can have on a person. He had bantered with people about religion all his life but never once entertained the idea that one of these reported miracles might have actually happened, and if it did, what the implications would be. He reached down deep for a clever response and came up with a rather lame one. "Well, those things just don't happen."

Charlene sensed the weakness across the room and went in for a classroom version of her volleyball spike. "Boy, I'm no Stanford philosopher like you, but to me that sounds like something you'd say around your surfing friends. I don't think you came in with a very empty cup!"

Another student chimed in, "Yeah, how could you possibly know that miracles just don't happen?"

Reagan weighed in. "Good question. That seems to me to be the real issue. We probably shouldn't just throw miracles out the window because they don't fit nicely into the way we want to see the world. If Jesus really did heal a man who was paralyzed, instantly and miraculously, that's a pretty good reason to believe he might be able to forgive sins as well. I think that's the point of the First Crossing: Don't just have blind faith in any spiritual ideas or statements. Instead, have good reasons to believe them."

Charlene reached under her chair and pulled a Bible out of her backpack. "You gotta hear this," she said. "The teacher at the college group at my church read this the other day, and it struck me as odd, but I can't believe how well it applies here. Just a second…here

Five Sacred Crossings

it is. It comes from a book called First Corinthians, which was written by the apostle Paul, who claimed to have seen Jesus after the resurrection. He wrote this: 'If Christ has not been raised, our preaching is useless and so is your faith.' Does that sound as odd to you as it does to me?"

Charlene continued, her eyes getting brighter as she talked. "This seems to be contradicting what we were saying earlier about religion being only about individual faith. According to this, Paul is claiming that if the resurrection never happened, Christianity isn't true, that our faith is worthless. He seems to be linking the whole thing to a historical event, something you can actually investigate. That's something even Darren could go along with—a religious claim we can actually check out historically. If that's what the First Crossing is saying, I can see why you might think it's so impressive."

Gyandev continued to whisper to Virginia intermittently through the whole classroom exchange. Michael wondered if Gyandev was giving her a running commentary of his views during the discussion. In normal teacher mode, Michael would have asked for their thoughts because they were obviously engaged by the ideas. But in trying to stick with the Cardamom way of doing things, Michael was purposely not inserting himself. Instead he let the "initiates" work through the issues themselves.

Then, trying to save face and get back in the game, Darren said, "I agree. If someone is making a religious claim that you can actually investigate, that's a huge step forward. But really, you can talk about resurrections and miracles all day. It's easy to bring up things that supposedly took place a couple thousand years ago. Why don't we see these things today? If these events are supposed to verify someone's inner religious experience, why aren't they happening now? The fact is that all religions claim they are God's special way or that they have the truth. But why do they want to keep us in the dark?"

Michael was again anxious to jump in. But he figured he could talk to Darren after class about the present-day miracles he had seen and experienced—extraordinary instances of supernatural knowledge and miraculous healing. He had once prayed with a group of

Christians in an illegal house church in China for a woman who had been blind since birth. She received her sight the moment they prayed. She and her whole village were so astonished that large numbers of people gave themselves to "Jesus the Healer."

Michael had also been present in a small church meeting in the capital of Ghana in Africa when a man from an outlying village carried in the body of his son, who had died the night before. The body was cold and stiff, but they prayed anyway. While they all had their eyes closed and their faces to the ground, the boy sat up and waited patiently for them to stop praying. The boy caught his father's eye when his father finally lifted his head from the ground. The father looked like he was seeing a ghost, but the boy casually said he was thirsty. They all asked the boy what happened, and he said Jesus had sent him back to tell people how much God cares for them. When word got back to the home village, people were lining up to be baptized by some missionaries who had all but given up on the region.

From where Michael was sitting he could see Gyandev tapping Virginia's elbow to prompt her to say something at that point.

Virginia stuttered for a moment and then said, "There's a way I learned to look at these things that has been very helpful to me over the years. One of my teachers used to tell a famous parable—in fact, it's in our textbook."

She put on her reading glasses and opened the book on her desk. Gyandev was leaning away from her now as if to emphasize that he was not influencing this. The other students didn't really want to watch somebody read out of a textbook, but Virginia had not said anything the whole time, and they knew she was a very sweet lady. They sat still while she read.

> Once upon a time, a certain raja, a king, called to his servant from the balcony of his palace, saying, "Come, good fellow, go and gather together all the men of the village of Savatthi who have been blind since birth."
>
> From the courtyard below the servant replied, "As you say, your majesty," and he went out to gather all the blind men from among the people of the village.

When the blind men were assembled in the courtyard of the palace, the raja said to his servant, "Bring in an elephant." The servant said, "As you say, your majesty," and he went out and brought back an elephant into the middle of the courtyard.

The blind men encircled the elephant, and each approached it with his hands outstretched to touch the animal in all different places. The servant then went to the raja and reported that the blind men had encountered the elephant.

The raja came out on his balcony and said to each blind man down below, "Tell me what the elephant is like."

One blind man who had touched the head of the elephant replied, "The elephant, your majesty, is just like a water jar."

Another who had felt the tusk of the elephant replied, "The elephant, your majesty, is a ploughshare."

Yet another blind man who had touched the leg of the animal said, "The elephant, your majesty, is just like a post."

One more had felt the tuft at the end of the tail and said, "The elephant, your majesty, is a broom."

The blind men then began to quarrel and shout. "Yes it is! No it is not! An elephant is not like that. Yes, it is like that," and so on until they began to strike each other with their fists.

The raja was delighted with the scene below and said, "Why do you quarrel and fight? If you were not blind, you would know that you are all encountering the same thing, but each touching only one part."

Virginia then concluded by saying, "I think that story says it all so well. It really speaks for itself."

Apparently, Gyandev didn't agree that no explanation was necessary. He immediately scooted his chair out in front of Virginia and said very authoritatively, "Yes, there is a spiritual reality, and it is very important that we all apprehend this reality in our own time and in our own way. Personal fulfillment and the future of humankind depend on this."

He had a very subtle accent in his speech that suggested he may originally have been from France or Belgium. The students were a little put off by his statement. They wouldn't have minded had he asked a question, but the fact that a first-time guest sounded as if he was preaching at them got their hackles up.

The class time was nearly over, and since a guest had inserted himself, Michael thought that it would be polite to get involved. So he smiled at Gyandev and addressed him in French.

"*Je détecte un accent très subtile. Je devine qu'il est de la France autour de la région d'Auvergne* [I detect a very subtle accent. I'm guessing it's from France, around the Auvergne region]."

"*Pas mal du tout. Vous avez une bonne oreille.* [Not bad. You have a very good ear]," Gyandev responded.

"*Ah, vous n'auriez pas du parlé en français parce que maintenant je sais. Vous êtes de Lausanne ou de Montreux, de la Suisse de langue française!* [Oh, you should not have spoken in French because now I know. You are either from Lausanne or Montreux, in French-speaking Switzerland!]" said Michael. He loved to guess dialects and accents.

"*Très bien, je suis impressionné. Je suis né a Montreux* [Very good, I'm impressed. I was born in Montreux]," Gyandev replied.

Reagan's father spoke to her in French often as a child. She may have been the only other person in the class following the conversation.

Michael addressed the entire class in English: "Our time is almost up, and I wanted to make sure I had a chance to tell you that your dialogue was very impressive. I'm so grateful for the participation. If you are left a little confused or unsatisfied, don't forget, according to the path of the Five Crossings, we have taken only our first step out of the dark jungle on our way home. So don't be discouraged. Make sure you attend the next four sessions to see how the crossings work on you and your understanding. It really is a remarkable process, and you should do everything you can to complete it."

He then turned to the side of the room and said, "Thank you,

Virginia, for introducing that famous parable into the discussion, and thank you also for bringing along your friend. May I ask you both a question, though? This is one that I have always been curious about involving the story of the blind men and the elephant."

"Yes, please," said Gyandev.

"Well, who is the raja?" asked Michael.

"What do you mean?" they said together.

"I mean, he plays a very special role in the parable. He stands above all the activity down below in the courtyard and can see it all with great clarity. He is able to tell those with partial knowledge about the true state of the situation. I've heard this parable hundreds of times around the world, and the raja is always the forgotten figure. But it strikes me that by any measure he is the most important figure in the tale. He is the only one who can bring full knowledge to the minds of those wrestling with different perspectives, those poor blind men."

"I don't know who the raja is," Virginia said rather independently.

"In my view that parable is actually a marvelous illustration of the First Crossing," Michael continued. "If we rely solely on our own thoughts or inner feelings about religious issues, we will be like the blind men, hopelessly locked in argument and contradiction. However, if we are able to find an objective voice from the outside, one who stands above and can see and tell us about the true state of affairs, we will have what we need on our first stop home. The question we should be asking is this: Where is our raja?

"Let's read the First Crossing again together."

Spiritual knowledge springs from within and from without
Where one is absent the other is void

"See you all on Monday. Have a great weekend."

EIGHT

THE WEEKEND TALK SHOWS focused less on the terror threat than on the perceived incompetence of the investigators. The local police, the FBI, and the Department of Homeland Security were all taking it on the chin. More than a week had passed since the domestic cell was discovered, and all the authorities had was one dead Indonesian, a blown-up storage unit, and another unit across town with serious radiological contamination. Two suspects were still at large, and they may have had the materials to build and detonate a dirty bomb—a doomsday scenario for any area at ground zero or downwind.

Without new developments to report, the local media started to give attention to the local eccentrics for which the beach city was famous. One group took out a full-page ad in the local paper, asking for Batman's help. They even rented a spotlight to reflect a bat signal off the clouds at night. An out-of-work actor claimed to be Agent 007, in town to thwart the plot for queen and country. Every evening he walked up and down the beautiful waterfront in a trench coat, asking people questions in a Scottish accent (he was partial to Connery's Bond). Of course, it is easy to imagine what he said when people asked him who he was. He also entered the same bar each night after his rounds, ordered a martini, shaken not stirred, and got fairly good at throwing his hat like a Frisbee onto the top of the coatrack by the door.

The authorities were actually making more progress than they were reporting. They had been able to extract some data from a hard drive they found at the storage unit after the explosion. Some of the data they pulled off was encrypted by a commercially available program. The FBI knew they had a shot at untangling the code, so they set up shop in one of the computer science labs at LCC and called in two experts from headquarters in Quantico, Virginia.

Most of the files were not encrypted, and the FBI was able to access a list of recently visited websites. After looking at the Web browsing history, FBI profilers determined that these may be serious Islamicists, not because they were viewing radical Muslim Internet sites—none were on the list—but rather because these were college-age men without a single hit on a pornographic site.

The FBI was really hoping to get more clues about people, plans, and potential targets from the mangled computer, but no luck yet.

Darren's comment on Friday about Michael's "geezer" playlist made Michael self-conscious about the song he was whistling, so he stopped as he approached the classroom Monday morning.

"Good morning, everyone. Gyandev, welcome back...so glad you could be with us again," said Michael. He noticed that Gyandev had switched places with Virginia, putting him one seat closer to the center of the action than he was on Friday. "I hope you're all ready for the next step along the path."

A student named Ryan Kwan raised his hand and asked Dr. Jernigan if he could make an announcement before they got started. Ryan was a member of the student body senate and did this in his classes several times a semester.

"Of course," Michael answered.

Ryan walked to the front of the class with a somber look on his face and a half sheet of paper in his hand. He turned and simply read the words from the sheet.

"The student senate is so sad and so sorry to tell you that eleven-year-old Zoe Basilides passed away yesterday at 6:35 p.m. from complications from acute myeloid leukemia. Her family wants to thank the students of Laguna City College for rallying to her side, raising money, and lining up to be tested for a bone-marrow match. You all took her on as a little sister, and your actions meant so much to her and her family."

He finished and sat down without saying anything else.

Professor Lightner encouraged all her students to get involved with the campus effort to help Zoe, who was the daughter of one of the campus groundskeepers, and most of the students had jumped in. Word had spread during the last few weeks, that she was going downhill. The news wasn't unexpected, but to finally hear that she had lost her battle was nevertheless distressing to many.

One student began to sob, so Michael led them in a moment of silence for Zoe and then tried to get them moving forward. But the somber atmosphere was probably there to stay.

"We'll follow the way of the Cardamom elders again in our exploration of the Second Crossing." He turned and wrote on the whiteboard.

The Second Crossing
Only one hope remains for liberation
The greatest of gifts must be free

After a few minutes of quiet contemplation as a group, Michael officially asked for their thoughts the Cardamom way: "Let us open the door to the winds."

No one wanted to be first after the news about Zoe, so the silence loitered until Reagan took a deep breath and offered a thought.

"This one seems a lot trickier than the First Crossing," she said.

"Yeah, it sounds even more mysterious," Charlene agreed.

Darren demonstrated again that he really did have a mind

for philosophy, and especially for unpacking a proposition. As on Friday, he dropped all surf lingo.

"I think the key to the aphorism is the word 'liberation.' All of these crossings have a religious context, so I bet it's not supposed to have a political meaning. It probably means..."

"Oh, no," Reagan Nguyen interrupted, "that was the one thing I thought I did understand from this crossing. There is no greater human longing than to be free from tyranny. My parents and grandmother risked their lives to have political freedom, to be free from the Communists in Vietnam. When my siblings and I were very small, my dad made us all learn and recite that famous line on the Statue of Liberty, 'Give me your tired, your poor, your huddled masses yearning to breathe free.' I'm pretty sure that's what the aphorism is trying to say."

Charlene didn't agree with Reagan but thought she'd have Darren do the disagreeing for her. "Darren, what were you about to say?"

"Well, that the religious context probably means that 'liberation' is a synonym for salvation or enlightenment. And the idea that it is exclusive—'only one hope'—seems to remove it from the political context because there are probably many ways to find political liberation. I don't know, I'm mostly guessing on this one. The next line seems to fit with that. After all, what would be considered the greatest of gifts, political freedom or religious salvation? I think it would have to be religious salvation," Darren said.

Gyandev launched into the discussion as if he were a longtime member of the class, this time without using Virginia as an intermediary. "True liberation is spiritual!" he announced. Of course, Darren had just reasoned his way to that conclusion, but Gyandev ignored that.

"Releasing attachment to the things of this world and elevating consciousness is the path to liberation," said Gyandev, and then he took on the role of a teacher.

"Let me tell you a story. In the last years of his life, Lord Shakyamuni, the Buddha, saw great misery in his land. Powerful new rulers were marching through and destroying villages. One even destroyed the Buddha's birthplace and slaughtered his people. King Bimbasara, a faithful student of the Buddha and a fair-minded ruler, was killed by his own son, the ruthless and aggressive Ajatasattu. The Buddha never condemned or befriended Ajatasattu for his crimes. Kings in those days customarily consulted with holy men for advice and blessings when they were about to carry out important military operations. When Ajatasattu sent a representative to the Buddha to ask whether he could expect success in an impending invasion, the Buddha said only that violence brings violence and peace brings peace. After that he remained silent."

Charlene responded, "Wow, I was having enough trouble trying to make sense of the Second Crossing, now we have to wade through this? I'm pretty confused."

Darren said, "I don't think what he said is all that confusing, I just don't see how anyone can support it. So let's say liberation is spiritual. Does that really mean that we sit silently while aggressive, ruthless killers march in and slaughter innocent people? That's not a very good advertisement for the Buddhist faith or whatever religious view you're promoting. Besides, I seriously doubt that's what the Second Crossing is talking about."

Michael was cringing at the exchange between Gyandev and Darren. He knew Buddhism had some serious conceptual drawbacks, but it deserved more careful treatment than that.

Reagan said, "I really do want to understand the Second Crossing, so do you think we can all focus more specifically on that?"

Charlene took a shot at it. "If liberation does mean something spiritual, then this aphorism reminds me of the idea in Christianity that salvation is a free gift from God."

"Yeah, but salvation from what?" asked Darren.

"Sin," Charlene replied.

Gyandev must have sensed that he was overstepping his status as a guest in the class because he reached over and tapped on Virginia's elbow to get her to respond.

"I don't know, I think the idea of sin is so negative," Virginia said. "Isn't it better to focus on the things that uplift the human spirit? The constant emphasis on sin has always been something that has turned me off from Christianity."

Reagan said, "I know we Catholics have our pet views of sin, but it seems to me that throughout this course we have learned that every religion has an ideal or a high standard that the adherents are supposed to meet to please the deity or to make progress toward enlightenment, and so on. It's one of those very few features that are common to all religions. Humans don't seem to be okay the way they are. They have to do something to achieve the standard or ideal."

"Virginia, do you believe in karma?" Charlene asked. "That's similar to sin, isn't it?"

Gyandev answered for her. "No, no. Sin is a very negative concept. It is supposed to be disobedience to a personal God. Karma is about education. Poor karma can build up when we perform actions that demonstrate a lack of understanding or knowledge. But the goal is all about growing in knowledge and gaining understanding, not stepping on God's toes and then paying for it, like sin."

Michael was once again cringing inside, this time over the ill-defined picture of sin and karma being painted. It reinforced his conviction that a good deal of interreligious conflict might be softened if people really took the time to get to know what the other traditions actually taught. It also reinforced his opinion that he didn't have what it took to be a Cardamom elder. He was always too anxious to step in and correct the craziness.

The initiate's discussion continued a bit, and then it was time for him to give the elder's discourse.

"The wind is now howling, and it is time to shut the door," Michael said while getting to his feet in front of the class.

"I'll try to bring some light to the Second Crossing—perhaps the most difficult crossing to translate into a modern religious mind-set. Let me try to grab your attention up front by saying this. The Cardamom never put an asterisk by one of the crossings or tried to play favorites with them. That would go against the tradition. But even in my brief time with them, I could easily see that the Second Crossing had a special place in their hearts. One of the leaders even said to me, 'If all Five Crossings are meant to bring us home, often when I meditate on the Second Crossing, I feel like I have already made it safely.'

"Now, occasionally the Cardamom elders would use objects of art and images in their discourses, so that's what I'll do today."

Michael was never on the cutting edge technologically, but he did stay current enough to find his way around a classroom or a conference hall. He pulled a flash drive out of his pocket and popped it into a laptop in the front of the room.

"Mr. Sosa, would you please turn down the lights?"

The moment the lights went down, Michael hit the button to switch on a projector, and up came a very crisp reproduction of a magnificent seventeenth-century painting.

"Who can identify the artist and title of this work from 1662?" he asked.

Three students raised their hands.

"Very good. It's by the Dutch painter Rembrandt Harmenszoon van Rijn, and it is titled *The Return of the Prodigal Son*. It's based on a story from the Gospel of Luke in the New Testament that has inspired hundreds of breathtaking paintings and sculptures and every conceivable type of imitation in storytelling. It has resonated at the deepest levels with every generation or people group that has encountered it.

"I assume a number of you know the story already. It comes from Luke, chapter fifteen, which has a very interesting context. Jesus is in dialogue with two groups of people who normally did not cross paths in that ancient society: the often self-righteous religious leaders of his day (the Pharisees and teachers of the law) and the immoral outcasts (the tax collectors and sinners). Luke, in my opinion one of the most accurate and significant historians of the ancient world, writes that the tax collectors and sinners were all gathering around Jesus to hear his teaching. But the religious leaders were disgusted that Jesus would receive these despised people and even eat with them. In response to this situation, Luke writes that Jesus told them a series of parables, including that of the prodigal son, which goes like this.

"There was a man who had two sons, and the younger one demanded that his father give him his inheritance. So the father divided his large estate between the two sons, and the younger took all that was his, packed up, and left for a distant country—actions

by the son that could be considered extraordinarily greedy and insulting in that culture. There the young man squandered his wealth in wild living. After he had spent his last dime, a severe famine came on the land, and suddenly he was in desperate need. He looked for work, and the best he could find in those dire times was feeding pigs for starvation wages—work that only the most desperate would take. He longed to eat even the garbage given to the pigs, but no one would give him a thing.

"As Jesus tells it, in this wretched situation, the young man finally came to his senses. He says to himself, 'How many of my father's hired men have food to spare, and here I am starving to death! I will set out and go back to my father and say to him: Father, I have sinned against heaven and against you. I am no longer worthy to be called your son; make me like one of your hired men.' So he got up and went to his father.

"At this point the parable earns its high place in the annals of storytelling. The young man deserves nothing. Justice dictates that the entire family and even the servants treat him like a beggar and stranger. He had his chance, he had every advantage a young man could wish for, and he threw it all away. He deserved ridicule, contempt, and shame for the rest of his life.

"But the text says that 'while he was still a long way off, his father saw him and was filled with compassion for him; he ran out to his son, threw his arms around him and kissed him.' The son, broken and weeping said, 'Father, I have sinned against heaven and against you. I am no longer worthy to be called your son.'

"This is the moment that Rembrandt captured in his stunning depiction."

Everyone in the class locked their attention on the screen in front. The image was speaking powerfully to each one of them. To be sure, something was going on in the room that couldn't be fully explained by the parable or the painting. If the students had suddenly shared their thoughts, they all would have been surprised to discover that most of them were being inexplicably moved emotionally and spiritually. A rawness and an honesty seemed to be penetrating normally hardened exteriors. Clearly, the announcement of little Zoe's passing set the stage, and the unresolved terrorist tension played a role too.

Michael sensed the dynamics in the room even though no one had yet said a word. He attributed it to the Spirit of God being present. He had seen things like this in religious settings but never on a secular college campus.

Darren Stevens had lived the prodigal life at Stanford the previous year, and his own father, a professed atheist, had embraced him and given him another chance. The episode was painful for Darren, but he had never once looked at it from his father's perspective. For the first time, Darren thought he was a lucky kid to have a dad like his. He clenched his lips together, fighting back tears.

Growing up in church, Charlene McKimmon had heard Jesus' parable read and taught many times. Michael's initial impression of her had been right. She had a deep emotional well that she was able to keep bottled up. The painting not only caused the soda bottle of emotion to be opened but also gave it a good shaking first.

Tears quietly streamed down her face as she stared at the back of the neck of the young man kneeling before his father. It seemed so open and bare and vulnerable and weak. It looked just like her little brother's neck when he was practicing piano. He was good at it, but she never told him. And the eleven-year-old struggled in almost every other area of his life. He stuttered, and he also had some damage to the peroneal nerve in his leg, making his left foot drop. Sports, skateboarding, and future junior high dances were not in the cards. Her brother certainly wanted attention, which was why he regularly pestered her. But that was also why she treated him worse than the family pet. She knew it was wrong but had no power and, even worse, no desire to change. She needed to become like a loving father to her brother, but she first needed to become like the repentant prodigal herself. The prodigal had no face, and that haunted her. She *was* the prodigal; so was her brother, and so was her own father, the globe-trotting preacher.

Virginia Renker couldn't get over the father's hands in the painting. She and her sister had been raised by a single dad. Their mother abandoned them after their father returned from military duty in the Korean war, causing a minor scandal in the city of San

Jose. Virginia's father wasn't equipped for the task, but somehow he found the tools to raise the girls with care and love even though he had trouble holding a job and struggled with alcoholism.

Looking at the Rembrandt, she could barely believe what she was seeing. The father's left hand was strong and masculine and had a firm, wide grip on the son's shoulder. The right hand, though, was clearly a woman's. It was smaller, narrower, and more fragile. This feminine hand appeared to rest with a very light touch between the son's shoulder blades. The key human figures in the painting were all men, but the father's right hand was a symbol of the love only a mother could give. No one else in the classroom probably even noticed, but Virginia saw it immediately because her own father had gone the extra mile to provide the female side of nurturing to her and her sister even though he was unnatural and uncomfortable in that role.

Later in life, Virginia's father killed a young woman in a car accident while driving drunk. He was grief stricken and died of an aneurysm during his third month in jail. Not surprisingly then, Virginia saw her father also in the position of the prodigal—in need of forgiveness and love but undeserving on many counts. If only he'd had a father who could have reached out and given unconditional love and redemption.

Gyandev Rose was initially struck by the message of compassion contained in the artwork. It reminded him of one of the great attributes of the Buddha himself—compassion for the suffering. But like the Buddha, Gyandev dealt with suffering by working hard at controlling his desires and emotions, so he avoided attachment to the image or its message. He was serious about taking all the right steps toward personal enlightenment, and in his view, too much reflection on the material world or abstract concepts like redemption, love, and forgiveness were not steps along the right path.

Reagan identified with the ghostlike figure in the background of the painting who seemed to be watching the whole drama between father and son unfold. Reagan was mostly a spectator of other people who were working through incredible turmoil, loss, and unforgiveness. Her own struggles with cultural incongruity and lasting friendships were real and often painful. But she also knew very well that her struggles paled in comparison to many in the Vietnamese community in Southern California who had at the center point of their lives a deep tearing and scarring over ancestors and nations and war and death and separation and anger and regret. Reagan was scarcely able to coherently identify the problems she saw, but somehow she knew that the answer was represented in the scene of reconciliation projected before her.

Even though Michael was describing some of the features of the Rembrandt, he was not looking at it. In some ways, Michael was extraordinarily brave for showing it. He experienced a double-barreled wave of emotion whenever he allowed the painting to work on him. He knew that showing it meant he might not make it through the class in one piece emotionally. He averted his gaze as much as possible so the power of the image would not overtake him.

He discovered the strength of the painting when he saw it in person at the Hermitage Museum in St. Petersburg. He had made plans to attend a conference in that city more than a year in advance. During that year, his wife, Susan, was diagnosed with cancer—a diagnosis that came only after the disease had seeded itself throughout her body. At her very first oncology exam, the doctors had the deepest looks of foreboding Michael had ever seen. The disease was inoperable, malignant, and lethal. Susan was dead within four weeks of her first visit to the doctor—a physically agonizing ordeal. Susan was a committed believer in Jesus and was filled with peace and trust to the end. Indeed, she even found strength through God to comfort those who, in tears and trembling, visited her in hospice care during her last days at home.

Michael was scheduled to leave for Russia only two months after the passing of the love of his life. A colleague in the psychology department counseled him not to cancel it but to go. Michael took the advice. The jet lag added to the fatigue and grief. Michael thought for certain he had made a huge mistake going. After two days of sleep adjustment he felt up to going with some colleagues to visit the famous Hermitage. Many of the works of art moved and inspired him, but then he came into the room where *The Return of the Prodigal Son* was hanging. The whole museum seemed to melt away, leaving Michael and the canvas communing alone with one another.

He sat on a viewing bench nearby and sobbed. He would lift his eyes for a moment to see the piece and then bury his head in his arms and weep some more. Some tourists gawked, but most ignored him. His colleagues moved on to different exhibits. But none of it mattered to Michael because at that moment, his Father in heaven was embracing him with one strong hand firmly on his shoulder to hold him up and one soft hand in the middle of his back, never to let him go. This same loving Father was the one who weeks earlier received his precious Susan into his presence with unspeakable joy.

"The repentant son, in the tattered and foul clothing of a pig farmer," continued Michael in his elder's discourse to the students, "kneels before his father with an outlandish hope that the father he insulted and deserted might offer him the lowliest of jobs among his servants. But in a startling twist—an unexpected turn, such as Jesus often used in his parables to illustrate the kingdom of God—the father says, 'Quick! Bring the best robe and put it on him. Put a ring on his finger and sandals on his feet. Bring the fattened calf and kill it. Let's have a feast and celebrate. For this son of mine was dead and is alive again; he was lost and is found. So they began to celebrate.'"

The parable and the painting were doubly moving for Michael because of something that happened in Vietnam. He was on patrol with his unit on a rainy afternoon when they began to take fire from some dense foliage up ahead. One member of the platoon had been hit, and the others were crawling on the ground, looking for anything solid to hide behind. Within seconds, the platoon unleashed a hellish barrage into the thick line of trees and bushes from where the attack originated. Then they held their fire and sat silently. They heard some wailing in the distance that certainly wasn't coming from enemy soldiers. The platoon moved in carefully and skillfully around the line of trees. They found one dead Vietcong fighter and evidence that others were there but had fled. Thirty meters beyond that, however, they found two dead children and one nearly dead farmer. The Vietcong sometimes attacked in the line of fire of innocent villagers so enemy soldiers would be reluctant to fire back. They miscalculated this time; the U.S. soldiers were not reluctant. The platoon didn't know a village was tucked behind the thick cover.

Michael's nightmares about the war almost always included this incident. He could never shake the idea that one of these precious children might have died at his hand. Over the years, people had tried to make him feel better by explaining to him that he was doing his duty, that terrible things happen during war, or that freedom carried a heavy price. And he tried desperately to let those ideas sink in to dilute the pain, but they were mostly ineffective. To him, his participation was like a stain on his chest that he couldn't scrub off.

Michael's spiritual experience in the Hermitage on that afternoon in St. Petersburg went beyond the comfort God was providing in the midst of his loss and grief over Susan. The stain of guilt and intense personal sorrow was somehow removed supernaturally. God the Father seemed to be saying, 'Quick! Bring the best robe and put it on him.' The same Jesus who had forgiven the sins of the paralyzed man had worked his miracle of forgiveness in Michael's heart. He was liberated from the sin and guilt that bound him. They would still be a part of him in some small way, but they would never again be barriers to his relationship with the Father, who loved him so much.

Michael had so much more to say about this, but he wasn't sure his words were necessary. The parable and the painting communicated more than he ever could. He knew the power of these fundamental truths, and he could see the intensity on the faces of the students.

"I know this is a fairly brief elder's discourse, but I'm anxious to hear what you have to say about the Second Crossing in light of the story and the artwork. So let me make it official by saying, 'The voice from the ages has spoken.' Oh, and it is the elder's prerogative to be involved in the final discussion with the initiates, so don't be surprised if I jump in too. Please feel free to share your thoughts," he said.

Michael asked for the lights but intentionally left the Rembrandt on the screen. It was still very much visible with the lights on. He thought the image had not quite finished its work on the hearts and minds of the students and guests.

The students took a few moments to gather their thoughts. Many were rereading the Second Crossing aphorism on the whiteboard.

Reagan was the first to speak. "The message of the prodigal son makes our first discussion about this Crossing seem rather silly. But are you sure you translated this correctly, Dr. Jernigan? It makes a lot more sense to me if the second line comes first: 'The greatest of gifts must be free / Only one hope remains for liberation.' In my mind, all of the emphasis is now on the words 'gift' and 'free.'"

Charlene had a lot to say about this but wasn't yet ready to speak. She was afraid she might cry in front of the class.

"If I'm seeing this in the right way," said Darren, "it's completely different from the way I've always thought about religion. The various religions always seemed like such burdens; you have to follow umpteen rules, and if you make one slipup, you're finished. For me, the idea of a loving father with open arms toward messed-up children is religion turned upside down. It's one of those deals where you want to say, 'If only it were true.'"

"One thing has been bothering me a lot all semester," said Reagan. "In order to really make progress in most religions, you have to have some special abilities. You have to be able to meditate a long time or have extraordinary discipline so you can follow a set of rules, and so on. Women or people of different color and nationalities are often excluded. But if the greatest of gifts is free, like this crossing says, and if what Charlene said earlier is true, that salvation is a free gift from God, then none of that matters. You don't earn a gift. If you earn it, it's not a gift. So no one is earning anything from the way they look or behave or the kind of work they do. If there's a tradition that offers a relationship with God as a free gift, that's a very attractive faith."

Virginia's eyes were still fixed on the father and the son in the painting. Something in the image was obviously challenging her beyond how it spoke to her own family experience. Michael could see she was wrestling with something. "Virginia, I'm curious about your reaction to the Second Crossing."

Virginia clearly didn't lean on Gyandev for her response this time. It came straight from her heart. She told the class the difficult story about how she and her sister were raised by a single father and about the tragic ending. But then she said something that captured everyone's imagination. "The Second Crossing must mean that there is a God and that God is deeply personal."

Michael was delighted to hear that. It was a point he wanted to make, but he was glad someone else came up with it independently.

Virginia continued. "In my explorations of Eastern religions, each one has had something that didn't settle well with me. Some, like Buddhism, are essentially atheistic. Others, like Hinduism, do highlight God, but God in their view is completely impersonal. What leaves me so dry in the Eastern views is that they can never have a powerful and loving being who can reach out in love to embrace them and accept them. If Rembrandt meant to capture some important attributes of God in the father of the prodigal, he really accomplished it. That's a representation of the God that I think many people long for. One who will accept us just as we are."

Gyandev did not look too happy. He liked to think of himself as accepting of all religious faiths, but he was actually a fundamentalist for his own view of the world. He was thinking that Virginia might need some special and focused teaching. She was obviously still programmed too much along Western Christian lines of thinking. Gyandev was certain about many things, but he was most certain that Christianity and Islam were two of the most serious problems facing humanity.

Darren responded by saying, "But didn't we learn that Muslims also worship a personal God? Given the fact that some of Allah's followers are plotting to take us out with a dirty bomb, I'd rather he not be so personal. I think this is a pretty good counterexample to the idea that a personal God is necessarily the best way to go."

Nobody stepped in to comment on Darren's remarks, so Michael decided to help. He said, "Darren makes a good point, but it's not quite so simple. Although Allah does have some attributes of personality, Muslim scholars agree he is very different from the God of the Jews or Christians. Allah has some personal traits—he has a will, he has knowledge, and he can communicate with human beings, although most Muslims would say he only did this communication once through an angel, resulting in the Koran. But in comparison to the God of the Bible, Allah is incredibly distant from humankind. We would call him exceedingly transcendent, whereas the God that Jesus presented is immanent, intimate, loving, and filled with grace and truth. Reconciling with Allah requires that at the end of your life your good deeds outweigh your bad deeds in the great scales of justice. Reconciling with the God of the Bible entails receiving his free gift of salvation and eternal life."

Michael turned and looked at the Rembrandt in a risky full and lingering gaze. He said to the class, "A piece of art like this could never come out of Islamic circles. Not only because images like this are tacitly prohibited by many Muslims but also because this representation would be so foreign to their concept of Allah. Allah may show mercy, but it's the kind of mercy a warrior might show someone he has beaten on the battlefield—he *may* choose not to slit his throat. What is depicted in *The Return of the Prodigal Son* is not a merciful father who spares the life of an errant child. Rather, we have a *gracious* father who gives unmerited favor to the wayward son he loves so deeply. 'Quick! Bring the best robe and put it on him. Put a ring on his finger and sandals on his feet. Let's have a feast and celebrate.' Those are words a Muslim will never hear from Allah."

After a brief ride on an inner emotional rollercoaster, Charlene finally felt safe to make a comment or two. "I can see why the Cardamom like the Second Crossing so much. The greatest gift, spiritual liberation, must be completely free. There's great wisdom in that. One big advantage I see is that if it's a gift from God, you can *know* that you have it. Does that make sense? What I mean is that if it all depends on our good deeds and our own righteousness, how will we ever know when we have done enough to earn God's favor? And how can we ever have access to the inner peace that can only come through knowing this?"

"That's the exact point the Cardamom made about this crossing when I visited them years ago," said Michael.

Charlene said, "I think I have a good example. Some Jehovah's Witnesses came to my house a month or two ago. I've seen a lot of religious people at church and elsewhere, and I can't remember ever seeing someone serving God with so little visible joy. One of my dad's friends was over visiting, and he helped me talk with them at the door. The Jehovah's Witnesses told him that true servants of God spread the good news door to door. In fact, they said, 'It's something we must do in order to be in favor with Jehovah.' My dad's friend asked them, 'How many homes did you visit today?' They said, 'Nine.' Then he asked them, 'If your hearts were truly in it, do you think you could have visited twelve?' They didn't answer him, so he just kept talking. 'Wouldn't Jehovah have been more pleased with you if you had made it to twelve instead of only nine? And what about your attitude, doesn't that count? You don't seem like you're enjoying these visits very much. Wouldn't Jehovah be more pleased if you did this all with real joy instead of grumbling hearts? In fact, maybe these visits are actually counting against you because deep down you have a less than positive attitude?' I learned a lot listening to the dialogue at the door. But the main lesson was that pleasing God with your efforts is a burden no human can bear, and at the end of the day, you'll never even know if you've made progress."

"That reminds me of a comment by al-Ghazali, one of the great thinkers in Islamic history," Michael responded. "After reflecting on the first four hundred years of Muslim history, he concluded two things. First, no one can ever know Allah. He is unapproachable and distant. Only Allah knows Allah. Second, Muslim leaders and thinkers in the early centuries of Islam consistently asserted that they could never personally know if they had done any kind of work, thought, or deed that would merit favor with Allah.

"Indeed, they didn't believe it was possible to know. They even hesitated to claim to be believers in Allah because only Allah could have such knowledge. This approach has generally continued to the present day so that modern Muslims are brought up knowing they can never be assured, not even for a fleeting moment, that they are on the path of favor with Allah. That's a stark point of comparison to the teaching of Jesus, who promises that we can know the truth and that the truth will set us free."

"Hey, do you think that's related to why some Muslims might give themselves up in suicide bombings?" asked Darren, not directing the question to anyone in particular. "I mean, if you can never really know your standing before Allah, the one you believe is the creator of everything and holds your fate in his hand alone, wouldn't you be prone to seek out the most outrageous act of belief you can get your hands on? Maybe they're thinking, *I'm never certain that my other good works are going to count, so I need to go for the grand slam of the religious world, the supreme act of devotion to Allah, something that will tip the balance in my favor once and for all!*"

Michael would have loved to hear the entire group engage on that question, but they were already a minute past the end of class, so he stepped in to wrap it up. "That's not just a wild guess, Darren. I think that goes right to the heart of the matter."

Charlene said, "That's what you were talking about on your first day with us. When we asked you why they wanted to kill us, you said, 'Because they have hearts that need to be transformed.' I think the Cardamom would agree with that."

Michael said, "It's time to go, so let's wrap this up by reading the Second Crossing together."

Only one hope remains for liberation
The greatest of gifts must be free

NINE

ON THE NIGHT OF OCTOBER 12, 2002, a young Indonesian man named Iqbal walked into Paddy's Bar in the beach resort town of Kuta on the Indonesian island of Bali. He set off a small bomb made of TNT in a backpack filled with metal shrapnel next to a crowded dance floor, killing himself and injuring a number of tourists in the crowded establishment. The injured and panicked vacationers from Europe, North America, and Australia immediately rushed out into the street. Fifteen seconds after the first blast, a white Mitsubishi minivan stuffed to the windows with ammonium nitrate soaked in fuel oil was detonated by remote control, leaving behind a meter-deep crater and blowing out windows all over town. More than two hundred people were killed in the streets of Kuta that night, including thirty-eight Indonesian locals and eighty-eight Australian tourists. In addition, more than two hundred others were seriously injured—many suffering serious and agonizing burns. The incident became known as the Australian 9/11—a wake-up call to the Aussie people and their government.

"Are you Professor Michael Jernigan?"

"Yes," said Michael while looking at the short man. He was probably in his forties with a loose Hawaiian shirt, blond hair, and an Australian accent. Michael took one last drag on his cigarette because he was about to enter the classroom building to go to his Wednesday class.

"Do you have a moment to chat?" the man asked.

"No, I'm so sorry, I don't. I have class right now," said Michael.

"My name's Rudy," the Australian man said as he thrust out his hand for Michael to shake. "Would you have time when you're finished with class?"

"Perhaps. Can you give me the quick version of what this is about?" asked Michael.

"I'm interested in knowing more about the Badui language."

"Yes, of course," Michael said with a growing smile.

Michael hadn't thought about that language for several years. It was an obscure language spoken by a few thousand people on the island of Java in Indonesia in four different isolated pockets, one pocket not far from the capital city of Jakarta. When he visited the country to lecture at the university, he met with the Missionary Institute of Linguistics and was asked by an Anglican missionary-scholar to help produce a lexicon and grammar of Badui. He worked on the project for several months and enjoyed it thoroughly. But they all had to abandon it due to unrest and threats in the region. Michael still had his notebook—a literal Rosetta Stone to this language—tucked away in his filing cabinet at home.

"I heard you were the man to see for information about Badui," said Rudy.

"Well, that must mean you're either a missionary to Indonesia or an ASIS agent," said Michael.

"Was I that obvious? I'm not carrying a Bible or wearing a cross. How could you tell?" Rudy asked. They both laughed.

"The Hawaiian shirt gave you away. Is that the uniform for the Australian Secret Intelligence Service? When I was in the army I did one job for the CIA, and they had me wear a khaki safari shirt. Can you believe that?"

"Yeah, those were the days, mate. Secret agents were supposed to look like secret agents."

"Well, I really do need to run to class. You can come sit in if you'd like," said Michael.

Rudy said, "I might as well. I'll just be sitting out here until you're done anyway."

Michael was serious when he said Rudy must be either a missionary or an ASIS agent. He knew those were the only two groups in the world who would be interested in learning the Badui language. Missionaries wanted to learn it, of course, for translating the Bible and teaching about the gospel in the native language. The ASIS needed to know more about it because radical Muslims had used speakers of Badui to make radio transmissions in the islands just before the Bali bombings.

Rudy followed Michael into the classroom and sat in an empty chair in the back. Michael greeted the class, introduced Rudy as a visitor from Australia, and immediately went to the whiteboard.

The Third Crossing
Everyone must paint a landscape
Eternal wisdom is with those whose eye is true

The students knew what to do and seemed to be getting better at sitting quietly and thinking through the words on the whiteboard. Starting a class that way looked a little strange to Rudy, and Michael's next words were even more strange: "Let us open the door to the winds."

"Are you going to show us another famous painting?" asked Charlene.

Michael didn't say anything, but he did shake his head no.

"I think I know what this one is saying pretty easily, but I feel like I might be wrong because they are supposed to be more mysterious than what I have in mind," Reagan began. "Isn't it simply saying that everyone has a perspective, or that there are many perspectives, but that eternal wisdom lies with those who have a view that matches the true thing…I don't know, I thought it made sense before I tried to explain it."

"No, I think you're right on the mark," said Darren. "I think it's saying that everyone has a view of the world and that those who have the correct view of the world have access to special wisdom, or something like that."

"I'm not sure that sounds right," said Virginia in a very soft tone. There was no visible prompting from Gyandev, who was in the same seat as last time, again a little closer to the action. "We've had a chance to explore a lot of religions this semester, and the one thing that was clear to me was that everyone has her way of viewing the world."

There was a pause while the students tried to figure out why she was stating the obvious.

After a moment or two of silence she noticed the puzzled looks and added, "And they all need to be affirmed."

The puzzled looks continued.

After another moment of silence, Reagan spoke in a soft tone nearly matching Virginia's. "I think I know what you're saying. You're saying that all the different views of the world are equally valid."

"Yes," said Virginia, "and it's really not very helpful or peace promoting to criticize another religion or worldview."

Ironically, the comment about promoting peace initiated one of the most lively dialogues the class had seen the whole term. Rudy seemed to enjoy it immensely. About a third of the class seemed to support the idea that we have to be able to criticize certain worldviews, values, and behaviors, or we'll have global chaos. Another third thought no one was in a place to judge another person's or culture's worldview or actions. The last third appeared to be apathetic, and a couple of students were passionate about their apathy.

Every cliché and worn-out notion about knowledge and morality seemed to make its way out onto the playing field in a philosophical free-for-all. What about the Nazis? How can you know anything? But can't we know that two plus two equals four? Isn't morality all about culture? One tribe believed stealing was okay. How do we know we're not in *The Matrix?*

The students who supported some kind of worldview critique seemed to be gaining an edge in the discussion. Gyandev was right in the middle of the fray but seemed to be getting more and more frustrated that people were not seeing things his way. After the debate had gone on a while, he'd had enough and said in an authoritative voice and with a heavier accent than usual, "You all must understand something. There are no absolute truths!"

The discussion paused again as several students looked at each other. Charlene, who any observer would have put on the apathetic team simply because she seemed a little bored, chimed in from a slouching, gum-chewing posture. "That sure doesn't make much sense."

Gyandev looked at her.

"If you so emphatically say that there are no absolute truths, isn't that really just asserting an absolute truth?" she said.

Darren was impressed. Another verbal spike, but fortunately this time not directed at him. "Yeah, philosophers call those self-refuting statements or self-referentially incoherent propositions." He was very happy to be able to show off some technical knowledge. The few days he actually did attend class at Stanford seemed to have rubbed off on him. "If you make the statement that there are no absolutes, your statement kind of implodes on itself because stating that there are no absolutes is itself an absolute statement."

He could see some weren't following him, so he tried an example. "What if I say that there are no English sentences? Well, I just used an English sentence to communicate that there are no English sentences. My statement refutes itself."

Darren felt like he was on a roll and making the most coherent points of the discussion, so he just kept going.

"It's the same thing if you say that all truth is relative. Think about it. If all truth is relative—that is, truth is really nothing more than each person's individual beliefs—then doesn't that mean that the statement 'all truth is relative' is also relative? It ends up being irrational and meaningless."

Michael was getting the biggest kick out of hearing Darren philosophize. The transformation this kid could make on a dime from surfer dude to Socrates was a marvel.

The guy sitting next to Darren high-fived him. Michael wasn't too thrilled with that because he didn't want the discussion to turn into a sporting event. He decided to intervene.

"The winds are certainly howling, so it's time to shut the door and move on to the elder's discourse. That was the most spirited and free-ranging discussion yet. Had you been carrying on like that in their village, the Cardamom teachers would have heaped praise on you all for wrestling so seriously with the topic.

"As you all have noticed, the Third Crossing can engender a seemingly endless discussion because it covers so much ground. You're right that it's addressing the various views of the world that each person carries. You're also right that this crossing is probably the least mysterious. Through generations of thought and discussion, the Cardamom have arrived at a consistent interpretation of this crossing: Everyone has a view of the world, but not every view of the world can be correct. Special wisdom is attached to those personal views of the world that most closely match the way the world really is.

"You can see why this crossing creates such huge discussions. You can have an enormous number of thoughts about the universe, and there is a very big universe to match them up against. I remember a peculiar example a Cardamom teacher used when I was with them. Suppose you deeply believe that monkeys are made of rice balls. It's part of your worldview. You learned this on the lap of your parents. Almost everyone you know believes this. But does your deeply held belief, your worldview about monkeys, match the way things really are?"

Most of the students looked amused. Rudy was snickering.

"The Cardamom teacher said that we all have excellent reasons to believe that monkeys are not made up of rice balls. In fact, we can say without any hesitation whatsoever that we know that the monkeys are not made of rice balls.

"Now this might seem silly, but we face analogous issues in our own experience all the time. I personally know great academics who hold endowed chairs at some of the most prestigious universities in the world who simply will not admit that they can objectively know that the students they are teaching actually exist or that the ideas and facts they teach are objectively knowable. I've met others who are utterly convinced that humans never landed on the moon. They believe it was a huge scam and hoax perpetrated by the government—I've never been clear about the reason why they think the government would do this, but nevertheless, they believe it.

"The Cardamom had a saying that was very helpful. 'We want to maximize our true beliefs.' I repeat this a lot because I think it is such a simple but profound idea, especially when dealing with world religions the way I do day in and day out. The Cardamom were willing to admit that their knowledge was limited, that many things could legitimately be disputed, and that they had to struggle to understand a lot of things. They had a humble approach to knowledge. But at the same time they were passionate about evaluating and testing their beliefs so they could be confident about what they did claim to know and could stand firm and unashamed in that knowledge.

"I kept the opening discussion a little shorter today so I can illustrate how the Cardamom approach the Third Crossing. They use what I think is a profound example: the problem of evil, pain, and suffering. Every religion and worldview makes claims about the world. Our job is to see if those claims match up. 'We want to maximize our true beliefs.' What do the various religions say about evil, pain, and suffering? And how do those beliefs match up with the way the world really is?"

The very mention of pain and suffering got Michael's mind moving toward his need for a cigarette, but he stayed focused.

"Each human being observes evil and experiences pain and suffering on almost a daily basis. According to the Cardamom, any worldview that does not do justice to these common human experiences should probably be carefully reconsidered. How do the various religious traditions explain these phenomena or make sense of them?

"Devotees of Eastern religious traditions, such as Buddhism and Hinduism, certainly encounter the same kinds of evil, pain, and suffering that other people around the globe experience—and thinkers and leaders in these groups have definite ways of plugging these experiences into their view of the world.

"Take Buddhism, for example. The Cardamom were very familiar with Buddhist thought. There are a number of different forms of Buddhism, and they approach the problem of evil in different ways. I'll have to make some generalizations, but I'll try to make the broadest representation possible.

"The first of the renowned Four Noble Truths—a cornerstone of Buddhist thought through the centuries in almost all its forms—recognizes the human plight of suffering right up front. The First Noble Truth states simply and straightforwardly that suffering exists. Psychological, physical, and spiritual pain is inevitable for all of us. Certainly everything in life does not involve suffering, but eventually no one will escape its grasp. The Second Noble Truth tells us that suffering arises from desire. We crave the pleasures of the senses, we thirst for what we do not have, and we desire not to lose what we do have. All of this craving, desire, and attachment to the things of ordinary life cause suffering. The Third Noble Truth is the truth of the cessation of suffering. Our suffering stops when our desire does. In order to achieve this, we must immerse ourselves in the fourth truth. The Fourth Noble Truth is the truth of the Eightfold Path. As we carefully improve our actions and attitudes in eight areas, the path toward the cessation of all suffering will unfold.

"The centrality of suffering, evil, and pain in Buddhist teaching is obvious, and Buddhism's commitment to eliminating these key human problems is commendable and attractive. What is less obvious and attractive, though, is just how to achieve this cessation of suffering. The majority of influential Buddhist teachers through the centuries have had similar outlooks on this issue. As we progress toward enlightenment, we come to understand that good and evil are impermanent and that we should shake our minds free of attachment to such concepts because they are ultimately empty.

"Indeed, as many *Mahayana* Buddhist schools have taught, everything we bump into in the physical world and even all the concepts and ideas we ponder are, in the final analysis, *nihsvabhava*—a Sanskrit word that means 'without substance' or 'empty of real existence.' This goes for everything you can imagine—flowers, electrons, love, speed bumps, the Arctic Ocean, stress, the Eiffel

Tower, and so on. Strangely enough, it also goes for you and me. You and I have no substantial reality either. That is, we have no soul or physical substance. Everything is impermanent and empty. In an ultimate sense, everything is *maya*, or illusion. To move forward toward enlightenment, we must increase our awareness of the emptiness of everything. In the final analysis, evil, pain, and suffering are illusions, and we shouldn't think of them as real."

The students were working very hard to follow him on these points, but so many of them seemed contradictory. A couple of times Darren raised his hand to ask a question, but Michael didn't acknowledge him. This was the elder's discourse.

"It's not that ideas and things, like evil and hubcaps, are worthless in Buddhist teaching. All entities, even if ultimately illusory, can serve a purpose on the journey toward enlightenment. Concepts like evil—and self and mind and existence—are all like a canoe at the edge of the lake. Once you use the canoe to cross the lake, you can abandon it because it has served its purpose to move you to the next point along the way. So, according to many Buddhist schools, evil, pain, and suffering are real for us until we obtain the level of spiritual insight necessary to fully understand that they are empty and illusory.

"I was on a television show once that must have been transmitted around the world because several weeks after it aired I received a long letter from a Tibetan lama, a venerable Buddhist leader from the Chinese side of the Himalayas. I had spoken on the show about the differences between Christianity and Buddhism, and he wanted to take issue with my remarks about the Buddhist view of evil.

"In his letter to me, the lama wrote a detailed discourse on his sacred views of knowledge, reality, and ethics. He then concluded with this: 'Evil and suffering are real only as long as the ego believes them to be real.' The lama put it in the simplest words possible for practical purposes. His solution to evil and suffering was to change the way we think about them. They will then cease to be real. Of course, he also believed that the ego, or self, was not real either, but that's another topic.

"The big issue for the Cardamom people at this point would be this: If a Buddhist holds to a view of the world that says that evil, pain, and suffering are just illusions and not real, does that view match the way the world really is?

"One of the most prominent ways that Buddhist and Hindu views on evil, pain, and suffering have been disseminated in the Western world has been through the New Age movement. New Age religious views are an eclectic collection of teachings from a variety of traditions but have relied most heavily on the Eastern religions and the more mystical side of the Western religions. From such a conglomeration of views, a surprisingly common approach to evil has emerged. This approach draws heavily from Hindu thinkers—such as Sankara and Ramanuja in the ancient period and Radhakrishnan in the modern period—but emphasizes proper mental attitudes and inward searching more than right action or behavior.

"The popular New Age view gives people a lot of control over evil, pain, or suffering. It all has to do with how one is thinking. According to this view, your mind essentially creates your reality. Proper thinking and attitudes will lead to health, wealth, and happiness. Improper thinking and attitudes, on the other hand, are the recipe for unhappiness and pain of every kind.

"What then is this proper thinking that leads to the positive outcomes in life? Fundamentally, it's the realization that you are God. You aren't a part of God because God does not have parts. You're one with the God that is all and in all. As Swami Muktananda, who founded Siddha Yoga in the United States, famously observed, 'Kneel to your own self. Honor and worship your own being. God dwells within you as You!' Once this self-realization comes into full bloom inside of you, distinctions between good and evil, pleasure and pain will fade away because you have transcended them. You'll understand the true nature of evil, pain, and suffering as simply illusion and the result of ignorance.

"Some of you may not be familiar with some of the New Age writers and teachers, but we're all familiar with Oprah. She regularly affirms for millions of her viewers this idea that ultimately each individual has complete control over life through proper thinking. Based on these New Age precepts about the true nature of evil, she has said during broadcasts, 'You can choose what happens,' and 'You are responsible for your life—the power of God is within you, above you and through you. You control your life.'

"Actress Shirley MacLaine was a popular icon of the New Age movement in the 1980s. She presented the Eastern view of evil quite accurately in her famous book *Dancing in the Light*. She wrote that 'Evil doesn't exist. That's the point. Everything in life is the result of either illumination or ignorance. These are the two polarities. Not good and evil. And when you are totally illuminated…there is no struggle any longer.'

"Again, in accord with the Third Crossing, the Cardamom people would ask, does this view of evil, pain, and suffering match the way the world really is?

"I did get to hear the Cardamom address this topic briefly while I was with them, and I think it's safe to say they would reject the idea that evil, pain, and suffering are ultimately illusions. Let me use an example the way a Cardamom elder would.

"Suppose we are going about our business in the class here on campus and the door creaks open in the back. We all turn and look to see an elderly woman with a cane making her way to the front of the room. It's an odd situation—random people don't just wander into class and have a seat very often—so we ask her, 'Madam, what can we do for you?' She tells us she has come to this religious studies class to tell her story. We've covered the important material for that day's class, so we say to her, 'Yes, please do tell your story.'

"As she begins her narrative in a fairly thick accent, we know we're in for a bumpy ride. She turns out to be a Holocaust survivor from Germany. In fact, she was the only survivor from her family and her village. Her family had been respected and upright merchants—pillars of the community—when Nazi storm troopers kicked in her family's door and herded them all aboard a truck. Her mother was killed on the spot for attempting to stay behind with the youngest daughter, who was very ill. The woman continues her story, telling us that on that night she was separated from her older brothers and her father as they put men and women on different trains. She would never see them again. They were packed into the trains so tightly, they had to stand for hours and even soil themselves because they had no choice. And the real horror hadn't even begun.

"She then recounts the humiliation, degradation, and slow starvation in the concentration camp. Tales of daily rape, murder, and forced labor. The stench, sound, and sight of ignominious death were ever present. Inexplicably, she was still alive, although just barely, when the allied troops liberated the death camp. She was the last of her family and the last of her village. She emerged from the camp, and knew no one. Somehow she was able to limp forward in life—a life that was denied to everyone else she cared about as a child. But of course she bears indelible physical and emotional scars. She concludes, 'That is my story.'

"Of course, we are all gripped and moved by this at the deepest levels because of the manifestation of obvious and overwhelming evil, pain, and suffering. Denying that such suffering is real would be unthinkable. It would be committing yet another evil and causing more suffering. Most of the Buddhist, Hindu, and New Age views are crushed by the facts of the Holocaust and other such manifestations of overpowering evil.

"The Cardamom didn't play games with such things. They made a point to face reality head-on. I think that's one reason they were so responsive to Christianity. Christianity has never denied evil but rather acknowledges evil and steps up to face it. Followers of Jesus, like me, still strain and wobble under the weight of this immense human problem, but at the end of the day, Christianity faces up to evil and points to a God who will eventually make all things right—a God who will wipe away every tear, right every wrong, and balance every injustice.

"What would Shirley MacLaine, Muktananda, Sankara, or Oprah say to this Jewish woman who suffered so much? 'Hey, lady, turn that frown upside down! Don't you know that it was all an illusion?' To put it very mildly, that is simply not adequate. Indeed, a comment like that would be despicable. Their view of the world is too weak to handle this weighty issue. It doesn't match the way the world really is.

"The Cardamom would encourage those who believe this to seriously and quickly rethink their views because no one can achieve spiritual fulfillment or balance holding to views that dismiss so completely some of these defining issues of human existence.

"I took a little longer than normal for my elder's discourse, and I didn't leave much time for further discussion. So let me stop here and close. 'The voice from the ages has spoken.'"

Gyandev did not look the least bit happy or amused. But he also was not offering a response. Virginia looked as if her loosely held worldview was undergoing a serious challenge. She looked pensive, troubled, and curious all at the same time.

Ryan Kwan, a theater arts major, was anxious to say something. "What you were saying reminded me of a stage play we're reading in my drama class."

Ryan had pulled a script out of his computer bag. "Check this out. This is from Jane Wagner's play *The Search for Signs of Intelligent Life in the Universe.* She wrote it for Lily Tomlin, who plays a bag lady with pithy comments about life. About midway through she says, 'I refuse to be intimidated by reality anymore. After all, what is reality anyway? Nothin' but a collective hunch. In my view, it's absurdity dressed up in a three-piece business suit...I made some studies, and reality is the leading cause of stress among those in touch with it. I take it in small doses, but as a lifestyle I found it too confining.'"

He put the script on his desk and asked, "I know this is a play, but Wagner is trying to make a philosophical point. Where could she be going with this? What is the alternative to *reality?*"

"Yeah, what do Oprah or Wagner expect us to do when we have, oh, I don't know, say, terrorists with potential weapons of mass destruction running around our neighborhood?" Darren added with a heavy dose of sarcasm.

Michael looked back at Rudy, who was following the whole class with fascination.

Charlene asked, "Are there really people who think the terrorists and their plans to cause huge amounts of pain and suffering are just going to evaporate or something if we say they don't exist?" She wasn't looking at Gyandev, but she cocked her head twice in his direction when she was speaking.

These questions and comments had the potential to make the

rather raucous discussion earlier look tame in comparison, but Michael didn't like the new tone that was developing. Luckily for him, the class period was nearly finished.

"I think I'll give Woody Allen the last word in class today," Michael said. "Woody said, 'I really did hate reality, but then I realized it was still the only place to get a good steak.'" The Third Crossing of the Cardamom wouldn't be far from that idea. They'd say that reality is full of bumps, pitfalls, pain, and disasters, but the great prize of eternal wisdom will come only through facing the world as it really is. Let's finish by reading together."

Everyone must paint a landscape
Eternal wisdom is with those whose eye is true

"I'll see you on Friday."

TEN

RUDY WAITED PATIENTLY WHILE Michael finished talking with several students after class. When he finished, Michael patted the pockets of his blue coat to make sure his cigarettes and reading glasses were on board, and he walked out with Rudy to get coffee.

Not surprisingly, Rudy led Michael to an isolated spot on campus to sit and talk. After some small talk in which Rudy deftly answered Michael's questions with nonanswers, Rudy pulled out a small digital recorder and told Michael that he needed help translating a message.

"I can't emphasize enough how sensitive this is," Rudy said. "A lot could be at stake. So before I play this, I just want your promise that you will not breathe a word of this to anyone."

"Well, first, I'm guessing you did enough checking on me to know I'm probably a trustworthy person, or you wouldn't be here right now. Second, I know how many people can understand Badui—especially in Southern California—and you don't have many options. Third, I'm a little reluctant to make a promise to a foreign agent, even from a friendly nation," said Michael.

Rudy didn't answer. He knew he didn't have anyone else to go to. After a quick glance around, he pushed play. Michael listened carefully to the thirty-second radio transmission. This was obviously not a conversation but a one-way informational broadcast of some sort. The voice was speaking crisply and without much inflection.

At this point Michael was in a great position to have Rudy answer a few questions. "Before I tell you what this is saying, why is an Australian agent bringing this to me rather than the NSA or FBI or somebody?"

"There's no harm telling you the obvious," said Rudy. "We haven't shared this with them yet because we don't know what it says or if it's important. We are certainly on the same team. Just a matter of agency policy."

"And why are you bringing it to me? Why doesn't one of your agents on Java get a native speaker to translate for you?" asked Michael.

"Again, no harm telling you the obvious. It's simple. We can't risk revealing that we have this to any unfriendlies in Indonesia," answered Rudy.

"Where did it come from, and why do you think it might be suspicious if you don't know what it says?" asked Michael.

"Nice try, mate. Can't tell you that part. Now can you tell me what it said?"

Rudy got another recording device ready to capture Michael's translation.

"I haven't worked with this language for several years. I'll need to consult my notebooks at home on some of the vocabulary. Can you give me a copy of the recording, or can I make a transcript?"

"No. I'm sure you can understand; I can't give you any of that. But can you tell me what you did comprehend from the transmission?" said Rudy.

"A few things. There were some words that didn't make sense. I'm guessing they were code words, even in the Badui language. There was some talk of money. And there was definitely a set of instructions or orders involved. Clearly, once it's translated, some deciphering will have to be done on the message," said Michael.

In a sudden and strange change of posture, Rudy slid the small recorder with the Badui message across the table to Michael. "Why don't you take it. Just don't tell my supervisor. Can you bring the translation and a report about possible nuances and alternate renderings by Friday morning? I'll be in San Francisco until this time Friday. Can we meet right here, same time? I'll certainly make it worth your effort."

Michael only believed about half of what Rudy was telling him. His one trip with the CIA in Vietnam decades ago certainly didn't make him a player in the world of international espionage, but a few things didn't add up. But the things that did add up seemed compelling enough. Michael knew that Muslim terrorists in Indonesia had used Badui communiqués in the past and that an Indonesian terror cell was discovered in Laguna.

What made it even more compelling was the part of the message that Michael understood but had not yet revealed to Rudy.

ELEVEN

THE MANHUNT FOR THE two Indonesian terror suspects first discovered in Laguna was going strong in several western states. Authorities were actively soliciting leads from the public. On Friday morning the network news broadcasts announced that an antiterrorism task force of the FBI raided a small home in an older residential area of Prescott, Arizona. The news anchors reported that a cache of explosives was found but that no arrests were made and that no details would be released at this time.

What the FBI would not be able to keep under wraps for very long was that the explosives they found were barrels of ammonium nitrate and diesel fuel oil and that the renters of the home were four Indonesians who were attending Prescott University. Based on fingerprints and descriptions, the federal agents were able to determine that the Laguna suspects were not part of this new group. However, the FBI sent word to every field office to raise their internal alert level to red and to drop everything in order to investigate Indonesian students, especially outside the usual urban areas. They suspected a network might be preparing an attack on several suburban areas simultaneously.

As Michael walked across campus to his classroom Friday morning, he was praying silently. He had fasted and prayed a lot on Thursday as he translated the Badui message Rudy had given him. Hearing the recording over and over again brought the gravity of the situation home to roost in a much more profound way.

Michael walked into class with a well-worn satchel that he usually carried with him only on international trips. Inside were his research notebooks on the Badui language, Rudy's digital recorder, and a single handwritten page containing the translation Rudy had asked for. He was almost unconsciously whistling "Someday My Prince Will Come" from Disney's *Snow White*. He had no idea how these random songs popped into his mind. Fortunately, he was whistling it very softly, and Darren wasn't around yet.

He chatted with the students for a moment to let the stragglers arrive. Not surprisingly, more students were becoming stragglers as Michael continued substituting for Willa Lightner. He wasn't diligent about cracking the whip on late arrivals; it wasn't in his blood.

Michael got the class settled and ready to start, but before he wrote the Fourth Crossing on the whiteboard, he presented a bizarre scenario to the class.

"Suppose you are an account rep for a big advertising company and are given the job of promoting a new perfume to the people of Laguna. You're convinced this product is so good that a lot of people will be sold on it the moment they smell it, so you want to let everyone have a whiff. But you don't want to just stand around assaulting innocent shoppers as they enter department stores. Rather, you, a budding advertising mogul, want to think much bigger. So you get your hands on a gigantic spray bottle that could put huge amounts of the perfume into the air. Here's the question. Where would you put the spray bottle so that you could make sure everyone in town had the best chance to sample the aroma?"

The students were slow to respond, thinking it was either a joke or that he was going to find a way to tie this in to some mysterious bit of wisdom from the ancient East.

Virginia finally said, "I'd put it up on Aliso Hill. There's a great breeze off the ocean most mornings and afternoons that goes right through the city."

Reagan, another local, agreed. "Yeah, that's where you see kids flying kites all the time. If you had a big enough bottle and squirted it at just the right time, you could hit most of the city, and it would probably carry over the low hills into the rest of the county. That's where I'd do it too."

Michael didn't give them a chance to ask him what the strange question was all about. He just said, "Thanks," turned around quickly and wrote on the whiteboard.

The Fourth Crossing
Wisdom does not live in two rooms
Knowledge divided invites shadows in the soul

As usual, Michael sat in an empty chair in the front row with the students to concentrate quietly on the aphorism. But he had trouble focusing. His mind was on the Badui translation and what to do with Rudy after class. He was debating whether or not he should call the FBI and was silently praying for guidance on that. After a few minutes, he said, "Let us open the door to the winds."

Gyandev was looking forward to today's discussion because the way he read the Fourth Crossing, it seemed to be very supportive of his own approach to religion. He was the first one to comment.

"This is, of course, the greatest insight among the Five Crossings," he said. "And I like very much how it is stated. It's addressing the real key to the unlimited self."

While he was talking, Gyandev was turning his chair a few degrees at a time in order to face the students. He obviously wanted to get up and speak to the group at length.

"Wisdom does not live in two rooms, and knowledge is not divided. Brilliant! Progress along the spiritual path is all about reducing ignorance about who we really are. Are we flesh and bone and blood and sinew? Are we organs and tissues and cells? Are we molecules and atoms and electrons? Are we an aggregate of pieces whose parts number in the trillions upon trillions? If this is what we are, there is no hope. We must begin to understand that we are not these physical pieces. If we can understand the truth—the truth that lies deep inside every one of us—that we are interconnected spiritually with every human, every creature great and small, everything visible and invisible, then liberation is at hand. This Fourth Crossing speaks to one of the most fundamental notions of enlightenment: my self absorbed in the infinite."

Charlene was in agony as Gyandev made his comments. She thought to herself, *He's self-absorbed all right.*

Darren liked having Gyandev around. Darren was used to eccentric characters because he'd hung out with his share of longboard philosophers who surfed Laguna. Gyandev was willing to say strange things with great conviction. He really stirred the pot. When Gyandev was finished speaking, Darren said, "I'm trying to get a better fix on what you're saying. Are you talking about the version of God that many Hindus believe in? Our textbook for the class calls him Brahman, and that Brahman is the name for all ultimate reality."

"I don't think you need to call it Brahman, but yes, that's what I'm talking about," Gyandev said. "If you would like it in more philosophical terms, I'd say that each of us, and everything that exists, is absolutely identical to Brahman or God."

Darren opened his mouth to respond, but Gyandev paused for only a second and then kept talking.

"God is pure consciousness. In it there are no internal differentiations or characteristics whatsoever. Ultimately we and God live in a unified state of pure awareness."

Although Gyandev's monologue was confusing to most of the students, it was helpful to Michael. With so many schools of Hindu thought, he usually took a good bit of time and dialogue to identify one particular tradition. The answers Gyandev was giving were pinpointing it rather quickly. His ideas were consistent with *Advaita Vedanta* with some New Age flavoring. This was the most popular form of Hindu thinking in the Western world.

There was a brief pause, and Darren took advantage of it.

"When we went over Hindu thought in class a couple of months ago," Darren said, "I just couldn't get a handle on why anyone should believe that ultimately there are no differences between things. It seems like all of life and every experience we have is based on differences between things and people and ideas. I went to a baseball game last night, and it seems to me that I wouldn't have liked it very much if the home team was the same as the visiting team. The pitcher was identical with the left field fence. The umpire yelling 'strike' was the same as a bag of peanuts. I need a lot of help understanding this religious view. It's not just that it seems like it might have a flaw or two. It's more like every experience we have in life screams out that this view just can't be true."

"Darren, you are actually further along the path to understanding than you realize," Gyandev responded. "The fact that you are asking these questions shows there are embers of enlightenment in your soul. So few people ever reflect on such things. But in order to fan the spiritual embers, you must devote yourself tirelessly to deeper and deeper levels of meditation. Overcoming the illusion of difference, the illusion of parts, the illusion of division, is not an easy task. Ask any experienced master. It requires a very serious commitment—perhaps over several lifetimes—to become aligned in mind and spirit with that which is all in all."

"Okay, then, I think I get what you're saying," said Darren, not knowing he was probably the only one in the class who did seem to get it. "But here's what doesn't add up for me. If reality is completely distinctionless and anything that appears to me to be a distinction or difference is an illusion, doesn't that mean that at the very center of your system is a distinction or a difference between reality and illusion? Can you see why this is just not plausible to someone like me? The system of religion that is supposed to display the ultimate unity in all things is actually grounded in a fundamental disunity—the distinction between reality and illusion."

Michael was again impressed with Darren's ability to comprehend and analyze such abstract material.

"Oh, but what you don't see is…" Gyandev interrupted.

"Wait, before you muddy the waters, let me try to finish just the most basic problems I've spotted in this way of approaching religions," continued Darren. Gyandev leaned back in his chair and crossed his arms.

"I think you'd admit I'm not yet fully enlightened—even though, according to you, I have some kind of fire in the belly. And I'm assuming some people somewhere have achieved enlightenment. If your whole religious program is basically helping people to move from a state of unenlightenment to a state of enlightenment, doesn't that again point to a fundamental distinction or difference right in the heart of the whole deal? It doesn't make any sense," said Darren.

"Yes, yes, these are common objections that emerge from the minds of people who cannot escape the bonds of reason. One arrives at these truths through seeing them directly or experiencing them, not through Western logical formulas," said Gyandev.

"I don't know, man. I'm not trying to be Mr. Logic here, but let me put it this way. I just can't get too excited about a religious system that throws out everything I experience every day and calls it all an illusion. Especially when on top of that, it has a couple of titanic, blastroid, ginormous contradictions right at the very center. Man, I think that would be enough to send anyone shopping in another mall or on another planet for religious truth."

Charlene was dying to leap in with her two cents just to join in what she perceived as a battle against Gyandev, but she had nothing to say. She didn't understand the dialogue well enough to make any kind of meaningful contribution, so she simply blurted out, "Yeah, it's obviously contradictory."

Reagan asked, "Dr. Jernigan, does this have anything to do with the Cardamom's view of the Fourth Crossing?" She was looking for a way to guide the conversation in a different direction. She didn't really think Michael would answer her during the initiate's discussion, and she was surprised when he did.

"The dialogue that Gyandev and Darren were having certainly has some relation to the Fourth Crossing, but I'm not sure the Cardamom would immediately recognize it," Michael said.

He stood up and then sat on the front table.

"That was more of a singles tennis match than a community discussion, but it was very interesting. The ideas were complex but well articulated. Why don't we call the discussion closed and start the elder's discourse. The wind is now howling, and it's time to shut the door," said Michael.

He was still working a little harder than normal to concentrate on what was going on in the class. He knew that once he started talking he would likely focus right in.

"I think the Fourth Crossing is a unique contribution that the Cardamom have made to religious thought. I've been thinking about writing an article or book on it for years.

"It's helpful to remember that when we interpret Cardamom thinking, ideas such as wholeness, balance, and completeness almost always must frame our approach. When the Cardamom speak of religion or the spirit, they have this sense that things are not right in the world, that things are broken, out of balance, and incomplete. Of course, that is not unique to them. Almost every religion recognizes that at least something is not right; that's why they say that we need salvation, enlightenment, or transformation.

"What makes the Cardamom approach different is that it seems to be much more consistent. They recognize the brokenness in the world that needs to be addressed, but they also recognize that the means to address the brokenness cannot also be broken. As they would say, 'One does not use broken tools to repair the potter's wheel.'

"Now, remember this principle as we look at the aphorism itself. 'Wisdom does not live in two rooms / Knowledge divided invites shadows in the soul.' The meaning of this crossing was not immediately apparent to me—especially not as a twenty-year-old army grunt. But as I later studied Asian religions, the meaning became much clearer. Throughout their history, the Cardamom people were surrounded by Hindu and Buddhist cultures. The Fourth Crossing is a response to these ancient traditions and particularly to the role of reason and logic in these religious views.

"The Cardamom recognized that Buddhists and Hindus, in their quest for ultimate oneness, were embracing ideas that were contrary to the very goal they sought, the goal of unity of life, thought, and spirit.

"You look like you're working hard to follow me, and I know this can be hard to grasp. So let me give you an illustration right up front.

"When I was in graduate school, I met a man named Dinesh, who was immersed in a certain form of Hinduism. He was born in the United States, but his parents were Indian, and he traveled to their homeland often to study under a famous teacher near the city of Varanasi on the Ganges River in northern India. Dinesh was fascinating to talk to because he knew so much about the doctrine and rituals of the sect he belonged to, and because he was born in the United States, he was able to communicate these ideas very well.

"One evening a group of us gathered at Dinesh's apartment to eat pizza—vegetarian, of course—and watch a movie. Afterward, we all got into a lengthy religious discussion with a lot of personal sharing. At one point in the dialogue, they asked me to describe my religious journey. I took the opportunity to tell them how years earlier I had become a follower of Jesus, how the living God had come into my life and transformed me, and how Jesus had opened my eyes to sin, salvation, and the true nature of things. I also told them that after careful study of Christianity and other religions, I'm convinced that there is no hope for men and women apart from the saving work of Jesus.

"Although everyone was being very kind, it was easy to tell from their faces that they didn't like the idea of salvation exclusively through Christ. Dinesh, however, seemed to be tracking with me. Even when I mentioned that the Scriptures teach that no one comes to the Father except through the Son, Dinesh was still smiling and nodding."

Michael paused to cough a few times. A small reminder of his bad habit. He cleared his throat and continued.

"I had talked with him in the past enough to know that what I was saying was not what he espoused, nor was it what his gurus in India taught. I was suspicious of his apparent enthusiastic agreement and asked him if he believed what I was saying. He replied that he certainly did. I became even more suspicious. I asked him, 'What if I had said that salvation comes only though an explicit denial of the claim that Jesus is the Son of God, that publicly reject-ing Christ is the true path to God?' Dinesh answered, 'That would be an odd thing to say, but I could welcome that as well.'

"I didn't need to ask him to explain. He could easily read the confusion on my face, so he began to give a mini lecture on how important it is not to fuss about the details of various religious views. He argued that all of these views were valuable because each of them represented a path to the same source of spiritual growth and awakening. Therefore all religious ideas and expres-sions should be encouraged and agreed with. Each one is a step along a different road toward the same destination.

"My first inclination was to argue with Dinesh over just how deep and dramatic the differences were between the competing religious views. But I didn't go there, and in retrospect I'm glad I didn't because the problem was not about the actual differences in religious views. It was about the concept of *difference* itself. Instead, I said to him, 'There is a very important reason that I would never be able to follow the teachings of your gurus in India.' I paused for a second, probably just to add a little drama to the moment, and then said, 'I just couldn't live a compartmentalized life like that. I really do have a personal drive to be holistic, and to build walls between different arenas of life is not attractive, and I find that to be an impediment to a vital spiritual life and outlook.'

"The discussion really picked up steam after that. Dinesh and his guests were especially caught off guard by the idea that I was claiming as a Christian to be more holistic or integrated in my approach to life and religion. Eastern religious traditions were supposed to be more holistic than Western traditions. Indeed, Christianity was usually considered one of the greatest opponents of holism. The discussion gave me an opportunity to make a very important point.

"I argued that embracing all religious views uncritically, regard-less of how contradictory they were, caused Dinesh and those who thought like him to live in two different worlds that were irrecon-cilable: the religious world and the world of everyday life. In their religious world, they can embrace contradictions anytime they like. The laws of logic—like the law of identity, noncontradiction, excluded middle, and rational inference—don't apply in this world. Dinesh is able to say that A can equal non-A—that is, a thing can equal its opposite—anytime we want it to. God can be the world and separate from the world at the same time. The 9/11 terrorists can be the righteous and courageous servants of Allah and evil mass murderers at the same time. Salvation can come exclusively through Jesus and exclusively through a spaceship hiding behind the Hale-Bopp comet."

Michael glanced at Darren, who was beginning to smirk. He was hearing this discourse, however inappropriately, as a kind of vindication of his arguments against Gyandev.

"However, I continued, Dinesh must live in another world, another compartment, where the rules are very different: the world of everyday life. In this compartment, all of us apply the laws of logic constantly—and this is no small issue. Our lives depend on us applying these laws properly.

"When you cross a street, it makes a big difference whether you see a truck hurtling down the street toward you in the crosswalk or a fluffy pillow. We can tell the difference because of the laws of logic. In everyday life, Dinesh can't claim that a pillow is the same as a truck and live to tell about it. But in his religious life, he can claim that Mormonism is the same as Buddhism. In everyday life we all have to make logical distinctions moment by moment, or we'll end up not knowing whether we are feeding our babies strained peas or transmission fluid. The stakes truly are very high.

"We went back and forth on these issues, and I finally told Dinesh I wanted to put my theory to the test to show him that he lives in two different worlds at once.

"I asked him to get his checkbook. He demurred. I asked him to humor me for the sake of the important issues on the table. Reluctantly, he finally got his checkbook. I asked him to tell me the balance—there wasn't much money because he was a starving grad student like me. Then I asked him to write me a check for that amount. He wouldn't do it.

"I told Dinesh that his refusal was an admission that he lived a compartmentalized life. After all, if his approach to reason and logic in the religious world were the same as in the everyday world, the money in his account would both be there and not be there at the same time. He could just assume his account held billions. It can all be true because ultimately there are no distinctions, no logical or financial rules that guide any of our thinking or actions or checkbooks.

"Unfortunately, in everyday life you can't make up the rules of reality and logic as you go. We have to deal with the real world.

"Almost every Eastern form of religious thought involves a dismissal of reason at some point, and that puts religion in one compartment and everyday life in another. The Cardamom people see that as hopeless, a path that will never lead to balance, unity, or spiritual wholeness. The Cardamom would see reason as something we must believe in regardless of the situation. Reason is the only tool available that can repair errant thinking. We cannot and should not discard or dilute it when we talk about religion. We cannot live compartmentalized lives and hope for spiritual fulfillment.

"The voice from the ages has spoken," Michael concluded. "We have just a few minutes left for our final discussion. I have to leave a couple minutes early today." Michael was anxious about his meeting with Rudy and wanted to have a cigarette first.

Reagan said, "I'm taking an anthropology class, and we've been discussing something along these lines. Human beings are called *Homo sapiens,* which means the 'rational, wise, or thinking man.' Rationality is close to the center of what defines us as humans. At the same time, other anthropologists have thought a better species name might be *Homo religiosus,* the 'religious man,' because you can't find a human culture throughout history that didn't have religion at its core."

"I don't understand the connection, Reagan," said Virginia in her usual soft voice.

"Well, both of these things, religion and rationality, are universal human traits. We even try to define human beings scientifically by these traits. I guess I just think it's interesting that the isolated Cardamom people understood this so well and were not willing to dilute or deny the most obvious aspects of human nature the way other more sophisticated cultures seem to have done," Reagan replied.

Charlene worked hard listening and trying to understand the earlier discussion and Michael's monologue, but something was bothering her. It was something Gyandev said, and it was especially bothersome because she thought she might actually agree with him. So she brought up the issue in a way that nobody could detect it had originally come from Gyandev.

"The way we've been talking about reason in religion is a little different from what I see happening in my church—and the people there certainly aren't Buddhists or Hindus. People are always talking about their experiences and how the Lord showed them something, or how the Bible spoke to them. You know, rarely do I hear them talk about *thinking* their way to these spiritual conclusions. It doesn't seem like logic has a lot to do with it. What do the Cardamom have to say about that?" Charlene asked.

"That's exactly what I was saying to Darren earlier," Gyandev blurted out.

Charlene was aghast. She obviously didn't mask her comment well enough to hide the fact that Gyandev already said something like it.

Michael was going to take a crack at the issue so he could wrap up class and have a smoke, but Darren jumped in. "Charlene, I think we're trying to compare apples and oranges here."

Charlene was praying that meant she was not agreeing with Gyandev.

"Just because people are having religious experiences that they can't explain or don't want to think about," Darren continued, "doesn't mean they think reason and logic don't have anything to do with their religious lives. I personally know lots of religious people who couldn't argue their way out of a theological paper bag but who believe a religious system should make sense—even if they can't make sense of it themselves."

Michael took the final word so he could call an end to the class. "I think the Cardamom would agree with Darren. It's not a question of whether or not you can make perfect sense of your beliefs at all times—I'm not sure anyone can do that. It's a question of whether religion should ultimately have any connection to rational thought. Eastern traditions have often viewed reason and logic as barriers to spiritual progress. Western traditions, on the other hand, generally embrace reason and logic regardless of whether an individual believer takes advantage of these tools of understanding.

"Hey, before we go," Michael said quickly, "remember that Monday is our last regular class meeting before final exams. We'll be covering the Fifth Crossing, so don't miss it. Let's read together."

Wisdom does not live in two rooms
Knowledge divided invites shadows in the soul

TWELVE

AFTER CLASS, MICHAEL GOT COFFEE and sat at the table where he and Rudy met on Wednesday. He lit a cigarette, pulled the translation page from his satchel, and read through it again. He was trying not to jump to conclusions because he didn't know the origin or context or timing of the Badui transmission, nor did he really know who Rudy was. But in light of the terrorist cell discovery in Laguna, he could still easily read a lot into it.

> At the voice of the Angel of God, *Subhanahu wa Ta'ala,*
> his servants will carry out his will.

Michael recognized the Arabic phrase in the middle of the opening sentence when Rudy first played it for him on his recorder. It was a standard utterance of reverence toward God that Muslims made whenever they mentioned his name. It meant something like "Glorified and exalted is he."

> God will meet the needs of [or give means to] the walking dead [the martyrs?] through his own storehouse.
> The entrance [combination, account number?] will be revealed in another voice.
> The sword will be [eruption?—not sure of word meaning here] and poison borne by wind.

From the [word not known—maybe strongbox or stronghold or strong pit] above the lagoon, the righteous judgment will commence.

From the west to the east in rapid steps, the enemies of God shall go down.

Make ready the lamp of justice, but wait for the voice of the Angel in your own tongue.

After these words, the speaker on the recording then uttered several sets of numbers. Michael wrote them down and thought the numbers would certainly keep some cryptology squad busy for a while—account numbers, GPS coordinates, dates, coded instructions…who knows?

Michael had a second cigarette, and still no Rudy. After a half hour Michael became restless. He looked under the table and under the chairs to see if a note was taped to the bottom—mostly because he was thinking about meetings like this on TV and movies. Nothing was there. He looked around for other clues or messages that Rudy might have left. Nothing jumped out. He waited another half hour and thought to himself, *Wait a minute, if this guy is really an Australian secret agent, why can't he call me at home? I'm outta here.*

As he packed up to leave, Gyandev Rose came around the corner, spotted Michael, and walked toward his isolated table. Michael immediately became suspicious about Gyandev being in league with Rudy.

"I'm so glad I found you, Professor. Darren thought you would still be on campus because he saw your car in the lot. I was hoping to talk with you. Perhaps I can buy you lunch?"

"That would be fine. I'd like that," said Michael. He was thinking they could get a sandwich and maybe sit at this very table. That would give him more time to watch for Rudy while they talked.

Gyandev peppered Michael with questions about his upbringing, education, spiritual experiences, and relationships. Although at times it felt like a mild interrogation, Michael was no longer concerned with Gyandev being in some sort of tag-team spy operation with Rudy. The questions he was asking were deeply probing but in a different way. He was looking for something, anything, that could help assuage some doubts he was beginning to have about real spiritual truth. Michael's own journey and the mystique of the Five Crossings had certainly captured Gyandev's imagination, at least for the moment.

Of course, Michael asked his own probing questions and discovered he was totally wrong on one of his assumptions. The way Gyandev interacted with Virginia made Michael think he was probably building a spiritual-romantic relationship with her to get access to her wealth. But he learned that Gyandev also lived in the tony Winchester Drive district of Laguna and had made his fortune by importing perfumes and then cosmetics. He sold his business a few years back for a hefty sum. He was about Michael's age and had the time and money to be a globe-trotter—almost always with a religious purpose in mind. Michael was a little embarrassed and ashamed of his prejudgment but didn't say anything to Gyandev.

They chatted for about an hour about their lives and about various religious ideas in some detail. Then Gyandev suddenly blurted out a question that caught Michael off guard:

"Where do you get your peace?" he said in his Swiss-French accent.

Michael was slightly taken aback by the strange question that suddenly shot across the table but then realized Gyandev had unwittingly left a trail of clues during the conversation that this was the real reason he had wanted to talk.

"*Comment décririez-vous votre père?*" [How would you describe your father?] Michael asked in French—a question even more out of the blue than Gyandev's.

"*Mon père?*" [My father?]

"*Oui, était-il un pasteur dans l'église reformée évangélique du canton de Vaud en Suisse?*" [Yes, was he a minister in the Evangelical Reformed Church of the Canton of Vaud?], asked Michael.

"*Non, mais mon grandpère l'était. Comment avez-vous su?*" [No, but my grandfather was. How did you know?], said Gyandev.

"I didn't know. Sometimes things just come to me."

"My father passed away when I was a boy, and I was raised by my grandparents," said Gyandev. "They were good people, but I must say that my grandfather was impossible to please. He was respected in his community and church—hardworking but very stern. I left their home when I was sixteen."

Gyandev paused for a long while. He was looking down at the table with his hands on his temples. Without looking up he finally spoke: "He tried to drown me."

Michael was stunned but worked hard not to show it. He had a very concerned look on his face but didn't say anything. He reached across and grabbed one of Gyandev's hands.

"He tried to drown me," he said again, much more softly this time while looking at Michael. No details provided.

The very sad moment of revelation was suddenly broken up by an annoying ring tone from Gyandev's cell phone.

"Oh, Virginia is out of her art class. I promised her a ride home," Gyandev said as he stood up, looking like his mind, his mouth, and his body were in totally different places.

As Michael observed the dramatic shift in posture, he thought Gyandev was probably very glad to be partially jarred loose from the memory.

Michael wrote down his home phone number, gave it to Gyandev, and said, "Call anytime you want to talk. Let's get together as soon as possible." Then he watched Gyandev walk away and disappear silently around the corner.

Michael was very solemn on the short drive home. What had just happened? Maybe two other times in his life could Michael remember having knowledge suddenly come to him like that—little truths that popped into his mind very naturally with a compulsion to say them—this time in French. He figured God would have to explain this one.

And what had happened to Rudy? With the Badui translation burning a hole in his satchel, he had decided not to wait. He thought he would call an old friend of his from graduate school. She, like Michael, had also studied Asian language and culture, but she took a government job with the National Security Agency as a translator or analyst or something. Her name was Josephine Leno, and she often signed her name simply "J. Leno," which opened certain doors of opportunity for her until folks realized she had the comedian's chin but not his sense of humor. Josephine had tried to recruit Michael soon after she got her job, but he was on a different path, and that was the last he had heard from her.

When he got home, Michael called up the NSA website on his computer. He went to the NSA contacts page and sent a note to the general e-mail address. He wrote, "Please forward this to Josephine Leno," and then decided to go for broke and tell the whole story about Laguna City College, Rudy, the Badui message, and everything else he could think of. The only thing he left out was the actual translation he had made.

He clicked on Send and then got up and put a load of laundry in the wash.

THIRTEEN

MICHAEL'S PHONE RANG AT three fifteen Monday morning. A few days before, he had sent a potentially alarming message to one of the largest and most powerful spy agencies in the world, so he immediately looked at the clock and reached for the phone.

"Hello?" Michael tried to sound as alert as he could.

"Hi, is this Dr. Jernigan?" said the man on the other end of the line, sounding much too cheerful for this time in the morning.

"Yes, who is this?"

"My name is Special Agent Schofield, and I'm here with my partner Special Agent Lister. We'd like to have a word with you."

"Yes, of course. I'm awake. How can I help?"

"We'd like to talk to you in person. Would that be okay?"

"Sure. How should we arrange that?"

"We're at your front door right now. Could we trouble you to let us in?" Schofield asked.

Michael hung up the phone, put on some sweatpants, and went to the door. After a quick look in the peephole, he opened it. Schofield was about six feet five and almost had to duck to come in. He had blond curly hair and a big toothy smile that never seemed to fade. Lister was only about an inch shorter with brown, neatly combed straight hair and a smile that likewise appeared permanent.

Both had on nice suits and ties with little American flags in the lapels. Michael thought this is what the enforcers would look like if the Mormons ever got into organized crime.

They held out their IDs as Michael invited them in. "Yes, please, come in, sit down. Can I make you some coffee?"

"No thank you, Dr. Jernigan, we don't drink coffee, but a glass of water would be swell," said Special Agent Lister.

Michael snickered as he got a couple of bottles of water out of the refrigerator. He thought again about Mormon organized crime.

"Sorry to visit so late, or early, I guess. We like to call first rather than just pound on peoples' doors at crazy hours. Makes it all slightly less traumatic," said Schofield. "We received your e-mail message and want to get a copy of your translation. It would be a huge help to us in our investigation."

"Wow. Showing up at three in the morning...something must be behind this after all. With Rudy in the picture, I didn't know what to think," said Michael.

"That's the other thing we need from you this morning—a detailed description and anything else you can tell us about Rudy," said Schofield.

Agent Lister was leaning forward in his chair, and his leg was bouncing up and down. He was obviously anxious about something but trying to keep it all under control.

Michael got his satchel and pulled out his translation page along with the recorder Rudy had given him.

"Are there any copies of the recording or the translation?" Schofield asked.

"No," said Michael. He didn't care because he had them memorized.

"Are you sure?" said Schofield. It was the first hint of mistrust or suspicion.

Michael nodded yes, figuring Schofield was just doing his job.

They didn't ask if they could have them, but Lister picked up the recorder with a handkerchief and placed it in a plastic bag. He then quickly asked Michael a battery of questions about Rudy's

Five Sacred Crossings

appearance and the conversation. Schofield was intensely studying the translation.

"Um…where you say 'eruption' here," Schofield said while pointing at the page, "what else could that mean?"

Michael said, "I really am guessing there. The word seems related to "volcano"—something the Badui speakers know well. There are ten to twenty volcanoes on Java alone. But it's a kind of verb form like a gerund."

From the look on Lister's face, he obviously hadn't studied grammar for a while.

"The context isn't helpful, but if I had to make up a word to capture it, I'd say something like 'volcanoing,'" Michael explained. "Hey, can you guys tell me anything about what's going on? Might actually help me interpret the message."

Schofield looked at his watch and said, "No, we can't share anything with you at this point. Sorry. Now what about 'strongbox, stronghold, strong pit'…any more help with that?"

"No, that's the best I can do," said Michael. "From the words I gave you, your guess is as good as mine. Obviously, 'strong' is the operative word. But it's clearly not 'fortress'; they have another word for that. It's something small but strong or protected, maybe like a safe or an armored car."

Agent Lister's cell phone started vibrating in his coat pocket. He didn't answer it, but both agents stood up suddenly, thanked Michael, and headed for the door—still smiling, of course.

It was now three thirty, and Michael was able to go right back to sleep for a few hours. Lots of international travel made him good at handling sleep interruptions.

Michael walked into the classroom just on time. He was glad to see that Gyandev was back and was looking forward to another talk. Michael's whistling was less subdued this time. The tune for the day was "Isn't She Lovely" by Stevie Wonder. He had nothing in his hands except a page that he handed to

Reagan. It was a printout of a photo of Willa Lightner holding her newborn daughter, Durga. Willa had e-mailed it to him over the weekend, and Michael wanted to share it with the class.

After a sincere, "Ahh, she's so cute," Reagan passed it on to the next person. Similar comments soon filled the room. Reagan asked Michael if he knew what "Durga" meant.

"I thought one of you might ask," he said. "It's certainly an unusual name for a girl in North America. It's even an unusual name in southern Asia. Durga is probably the fiercest goddess in the Hindu pantheon; her name in Sanskrit means 'invincible.' In Indian art she is usually seen holding every weapon imaginable and riding a lion or a tiger. In early Hindu mythology she is the goddess who dances on the corpse of the dead male god Siva, who tradition says created her in the first place."

The "aahs" in the class turned to "oohs" as the radical feminist implications of the name dawned on the students.

"Before we start, let me ask you all another strange question. I suppose this is most directly pointed at those of you who grew up in Laguna. What landmark would remind you of a strongbox or a strong pit? I know that's a very strange question, but do those words conjure up something that you know about in town or nearby?"

Ryan raised his hand right away and said, "Yeah, that reminds me of the vault at Coastal Savings and Loan, where I worked last year. I heard the manager say they had the biggest vault in town."

Another student answered, "You said 'pit'? There's a small garbage pit used by some families just north of the city limits. I did a story on them for my high school newspaper. Years ago they were able to get a judge to exempt them from trash collection fees. It's not really 'strong' unless you mean smell, and I'm not so sure it's a landmark."

"That makes me think of the pillbox," said Darren.

"Hey, yeah, I forgot about that," said Ryan. "That was kinda before our time."

"What's the pillbox?" asked Reagan.

Ryan Kwan said, "My dad told me about some World War II bunkers on a few hills along the coast. They were concrete lookout posts. You know, to watch for Japanese subs, airplanes, and commandos, things like that. Of course, they were abandoned after the war, but in my dad's day, the local pillbox was party central. The sheriff finally had the openings to the thing blocked up with cement. Then they bulldozed dirt over the parts that were still visible and really messed up the dirt road that led up there. My dad showed me once where it was."

"Yeah, I heard one of the geezer surfers point up there from the water and talk about his partyin' at the pillbox," said Darren.

"So where is it?" asked Reagan.

"It's just above the park where people fly kites. You know, up on Aliso Hill," said Ryan.

A wave of alarm hit Michael the moment Ryan mentioned Aliso Hill, but he tried not to show it in his demeanor. In his mind, in his spirit, the alarm was more than the apparent alignment of some circumstantial evidence. He'd felt this several times in his life—twice in Vietnam. It was like God's Spirit signaling his spirit that he should be especially alert and prepared. Ironically, the feeling was calming because it was strong evidence that he was not alone, that God knew his name and had numbered every hair on his head.

Michael asked if he could borrow Reagan's cell phone. He went out of the room and down the hall, pulled Agent Schofield's business card out of his wallet, and dialed the number. His call immediately went to voice mail, so Michael left a message.

"This is Michael Jernigan. Please call me back on this phone when you get this message. I may have some very important information for the terror investigation. I'll be in class at LCC, but I'll make sure we pick up when you call. Thanks."

He walked back in the classroom, gave the phone back to Reagan, and asked if she wouldn't mind if he got a return call. He had her turn the ringer on high.

"Please forgive me for the interruption, especially during our last session together. Why don't we get started," Michael said to the class.

Charlene had a funny smile on her face while she was chewing her gum. "We're way ahead of you," she said, pointing to the whiteboard behind Michael, where she had written the Fifth Crossing. "And we all agree that my handwriting's a lot better than yours."

Michael pulled up a chair, and they all gave the aphorism a couple of minutes of undivided attention.

The Fifth Crossing

The one who transcends boundaries
Is he who brings deliverance

"Let us open the door to the winds," said Michael.

Virginia seemed to be gaining confidence because she didn't even look around to see if anyone else was gearing up for a comment. She just stepped up and kicked off the discussion.

"I'm a member of a spiritual reading group, and last year we all read through a book about the *Maitreya*, a great world teacher that most of the world's religions talk about. The Fifth Crossing is amazing to me because it shows that an isolated group in Cambodia was welling up with anticipation of this coming teacher as well. Earlier this year we read a book about Carl Jung, who taught on things he called 'archetypes of the collective unconscious.' These archetypes show that humans through the ages have had a common psychic experience. Jung taught that we can better understand the common experiences and spiritual core of all human beings by looking at the symbols that have emerged through human art, dreams, and religion. I'm sorry, I probably went on too long. But that's what this crossing made me think of."

Michael wanted to say, "No, no, that was very well said," in order to encourage Virginia, but he stayed true to his role and didn't say anything.

Reagan said, "This might overlap with what Virginia was saying, but I was struck by the focal point of the Fifth Crossing. It's the only one that sounds like it is talking directly about God or some kind of person. It says 'the *one* who transcends,' and then, '*he* who brings.' It seems like it's either talking about God or some *maître d*', like Virginia was saying."

"That was *Maitreya*," Gyandev barked out quickly and with a much heavier accent than usual.

"Gesundheit," Charlene replied.

Gyandev looked annoyed. He also looked like he might have a hangover.

Ryan said, "This is definitely messianic. Like they're waiting for a deliverer or savior. That's a pretty common theme in religious lore, isn't it?"

"Yes, this is right. Humans have always been anticipating a deliverer," said Gyandev. "It's part of most of the great fairy tales and most of the enduring religions. Sleeping Beauty awaits her Prince. Shiite Muslims look forward to the coming of the Twelfth Imam, and the Sunnis look for the *Mahdi* to bring in the era of peace and justice. Hindus watch for the tenth avatar of Vishnu, Christians for the return of Christ, Jews for their messiah, and Buddhists for the great bodhisattva and world teacher, *Maitreya,* as Virginia has already told us."

Michael listened and wondered if Gyandev was using dogmatic statements to cover up his own deep-seated doubts.

"What about where it says 'transcends boundaries'?" Reagan asked, addressing no one in particular. "Are there any clues to what that means?"

"I don't know, but my first impression of this crossing is that it plants you firmly back in religion land," Darren lamented. "We're back to a focus on God or a future savior. I liked the other crossings because for me they seemed to be breathing some new life into the subject of religion—as if the Cardamom people really wanted it all to make sense, like they wanted satisfied minds along with satisfied souls or spirits or whatever."

Darren had taken the discussion away from Reagan's question, so she asked it again. "But what about the phrase 'transcends boundaries'? Any thoughts?"

Reagan was again throwing the query out to the whole group, but Darren thought she was asking him.

"I can only guess at what 'boundaries' might mean, but the fact that they would be looking for 'one who transcends'—you know, some person up above—makes some religious sense," he said.

Darren paused for a second to think and then continued. "You know, this could really apply to the movie *The Matrix.* I watched it again at a friend's place this weekend. So here's Neo, the Keanu Reeves character, who finally breaks out of the cyber world into reality. He kind of stands above the artificial world and interacts with it as a sort of deliverer. I guess the boundary would be the border between the two worlds."

Charlene said, "If the boundary can be just about anything, then I think the story of the blind men and the elephant would work too. Remember when the raja comes out on the balcony above the courtyard to tell the blind men that the thing they're all touching is really an elephant? That has a kind of boundary—the one between the balcony and the courtyard. And it has transcendence—the raja stands above and sees all."

"I suppose everyone is looking for that voice from above, even some of the greatest philosophers," Darien said. "Plato was probably the greatest philosopher in human history, but even he got to a point where he threw up his hands in frustration. In the *Phaedo* he said, 'If only I had a raft of revelation to carry me over the seas of doubt.' Plato knew he was limited and was desperate for a sure word from a transcendent source."

Some of the students thought they were on a roll and making progress. Michael thought they were getting off track with regard to the Fifth Crossing.

"It's really much simpler than that," Michael said suddenly, surprising the students and himself a little bit too. Once he said it, Michael realized that his interruption was a pretty good sign that he was a lot more anxious about the events on the outside of class than he was aware of.

"You're making some very interesting comments, but I think it's mostly my fault that you're missing an important point. So if I can give a word or two of explanation about the translation, I think I can help," he said, looking around the room to see if there were any objections.

"Look at the verbs 'transcends' and 'brings.' You were thinking of them as future tenses and that they were referring to one who will someday transcend boundaries and who will eventually bring deliverance. It's easy to interpret English verbs like these in the future tense in certain contexts. But they are definitely not in the future tense in the Cardamom language. They are supposed to be read in the present perfect progressive tense," Michael said, thinking that would clear everything up.

He got mostly blank stares. Even after years of teaching, he often forgot that most students don't know grammar terms.

"In this case the verbs should be read like this."

Michael went to the whiteboard and wrote underneath Charlene's lovely script:

> The one who has been transcending boundaries
> Is he who has been bringing deliverance

"It's not as pretty as the first translation, but it might communicate more accurately," he said.

"Oh, it's past tense. That does make a difference," said Charlene.

"No, no. It's present perfect progressive. Well, you know what, for our purposes we can call it past tense because the important thing is that it already happened. Sorry for the confusion," Michael said.

Virginia said, "So the Cardamom are not looking for a future deliverer; they're looking for one who has already come."

"Yes, and one who will continue to deliver. But what else?" Michael prompted.

"Um…it gives a point of identification," Charlene said. "If we can identify the one who has been transcending boundaries, we'll know who the deliverer is."

"See, it's really very simple. Sorry to complicate it earlier. But I really did like your conversation about Neo and Plato and *Maitreya* and everybody; very interesting stuff," Michael said.

"So who is it?" asked Reagan.

"Now that would not be very Cardamom of me to just blurt out an answer, would it? That sounds a little hypocritical because it wasn't very Cardamom of me to interrupt the initiates' discussion either. I know that at least a few of you know the answer to this, so why don't I just step out of the way and let you finish," Michael replied.

The students were quiet as they looked at the ceiling, bit on the ends of their pens, and twirled their hair in their fingers. More than a few of them had a strong idea because of something Michael had said when he told the story of the Cardamom people in an earlier class. But a lot of information had been swirling around them since that time, and they were trying to sort it out. No one was ready yet to try an answer.

Finally, someone spoke.

"I think I know who it is. I can't imagine another possibility according to the words of the Fifth Crossing. It would have to be Jesus." Gyandev's tone was unexpectedly unpretentious.

At the sound of his voice, the hair on Charlene's neck stood at full attention. It relaxed a little when she heard what he was saying. She was withholding judgment for a moment or two.

"Since this is a religious context," Gyandev continued, "I assume the boundaries it speaks of are religious boundaries—although I suppose they could be geographical boundaries too since it would work out the same way. Jesus is the only one I can think of who is respected in all the major religious traditions. In that sense, he transcends boundaries."

Charlene relaxed even further.

Darren was skeptical. "We're on the last day of a survey course on world religions. It seems pretty implausible that if Jesus were an important person in all of the religions, that wouldn't have been mentioned in textbooks or the lectures somewhere along the way."

Michael was taken aback. This was never mentioned in class or in the textbook in a serious college-level class in world religions? It was one of the most remarkable facts in the comparative study of religion.

"We took that field trip to the Buddhist temple earlier this semester. I didn't see any crosses or statues of Jesus. No one there mentioned his name or anything about him," Darren added.

"Did you ask them?" Gyandev asked.

"No," said Charlene answering for Darren. "I would have remembered him doing that."

"I'll bet you went to the San Clemente Temple, didn't you?" Gyandev said.

Several heads nodded yes, and Gyandev continued.

"I have had several talks with leaders down there, Darren, and I have been amazed at their deep respect and reverence for Jesus and his teachings. One master at the temple believes that Jesus is one of the greatest bodhisattvas—that's an enlightened being who stepped back from Nirvana to help others along the path. Another temple teacher actually believes that because of his compassion and enduring lessons, Jesus was very likely a reincarnation of the Buddha himself."

"Several years ago I signed up for a special spiritual tour of India," said Virginia. "We visited a whole range of holy sites in that country and had special meetings with esteemed religious leaders and teachers. A Christian couple in our group—a Methodist minister and her husband—asked the various teachers about their views of Jesus. The couple was surprised, as was I, to discover how important they thought Jesus was. They studied Jesus' teachings and some believed him to be a great yogi. One thought Jesus to be an avatar or incarnation of the Hindu god Vishnu. The high place Jesus held in their minds really was remarkable."

When Virginia was finished there was a slight pause and Michael stood up. "I know our system has broken down a little bit today, but let's officially call the initiates' discussion to a close. The wind is now howling, and it's time to shut the door."

"Oh, it's sad to hear that for the last time," said Reagan. "I'm really gonna miss these meetings."

Michael added, "I'm not going to do a full-blown elder's discourse this time. I'd rather just join you in your discussion to wrap up our weeks together."

Darren didn't waste any time. "Then Dr. J., what about Islam? I can understand Jesus being considered a player by people from Eastern religious groups. They seem to be open to almost any kind of spiritual teaching. But not Muslims. They have a much tighter system. It doesn't seem like they'd be anxious to make another religion's savior part of their deal."

Charlene raised her hand in response, and Michael let her make a comment first.

"We had a former Muslim come talk to the college group at

church. He said that when he wants to share his faith with Muslims, he simply starts talking about Jesus because Muslims have such a high regard for him. Dr. Jernigan, is this true? This guy said that in the Koran, Jesus could actually be considered greater than Muhammad himself. He said that the Koran says that Jesus was born of a virgin, he was a prophet, he was a miracle worker, and he'll play an important role on judgment day."

"That former Muslim got it right," Michael replied. "It's not that these other great religions simply think that 'Jesus is just all right with me,' like in that Doobie Brothers song. They really want to make him one of their own. In my view, Gyandev nailed it. Jesus really is the only candidate for a universal religious figure."

Michael sat on the table in the front. "Now of course, there's a real danger here of capturing the wrong point. I haven't heard anyone saying that the Buddhists, Hindus, Muslims, New Agers, or any other religious group has accepted without qualification the Jesus who is presented in the New Testament. As a follower of Jesus myself and a man who knows something about these other traditions, I can say with some authority that they do not generally accept Jesus as the unique Son of God, the exclusive savior of the world, and so on. But that's not the point."

He stood up again and took a marking pen up to the whiteboard and underlined the words of the aphorism written there.

"According to the Cardamom, the Fifth Crossing makes a simple point. If there is a deliverer for humankind, he will be significant across religious boundaries. I had the privilege of hearing Master Map Nuth himself give an elder's discourse on this topic. He believed the deliverer would live a life or speak a message that would address the deepest longings of every human heart. This deliverer would transcend boundaries of all types and would be accepted to some degree in all of the great traditions."

He put the pen down and sat back on the front desk.

"Remember on one of the first days of class when I told you I had met missionaries in Thailand who told me about the Cardamom people opening their hearts to the Gospel of John and then the person of Jesus?" Michael asked the students.

They nodded yes.

"The missionaries told me something very strange. They said that as the people were learning about Jesus, they kept asking questions like 'Is he known in other lands?' 'Do the Buddhists know him?' 'Is he esteemed in other villages?' When they discovered the answer was yes, they were filled with joy. Jesus fit all Five Crossings."

Charlene raised her hand lazily with a finger protruding.

"Yes, Charlene," Michael said.

Instead of answering, she just moved her hand back and forth, pointing with her finger.

Michael turned to the door at the front of the room and saw Dr. Gelman, the chair of the department, leaning in and waving to get Michael's attention. Michael walked over to see him.

"I'm so sorry to bother you, Dr. Jernigan," Gelman said in a very low tone, "but two men need you to come with them right away. Seems there's been an accident. Someone in the family."

Michael's heart skipped a beat, wondering who it could be.

"Where are they—the men who want to see me, I mean?"

"They're right outside the front entrance of the building," said Gelman.

Michael grabbed Gelman's arm and said, "Could you please tell the students I had to run off suddenly? Tell them how much I enjoyed being with them and that I'm going to miss them."

"I sure will. Please just go, and I'll take care of things here," said Gelman.

Michael patted the pockets of his blue jacket to make sure he had the essentials and strode quickly down the hall.

When he got to the entrance of the building, he pushed the glass door open, looked both ways, and saw only one man standing behind a park bench five yards away. He was medium height and was wearing a tan sport coat and sunglasses. When the man saw Michael, he walked out from behind the bench to meet him. Then Michael noticed something odd, even for a college campus. The man's pants were combat fatigues, and he had black military boots on. He also had a terrible case of hat hair.

"Dr. Jernigan, sir," the man said, holding out his hand to shake Michael's. "Please come with me, sir. We have a situation and need your help."

Michael was relieved that relatives were not injured, but he thought that might be a ruse. He followed the oddly dressed man toward the parking lot. As they rounded the corner, a blond man in a casual shirt strode out very quickly from the corner of the building to walk with them.

"G'day, Michael."

"Hello, Rudy."

FOURTEEN

"I'LL BET YOU HAVE a lot of questions," Rudy said, "but let's talk in the vehicle."

He opened the door of a black SUV with dark tinted windows that had the engine running. Inside were three more men dressed in combat fatigues with helmets and no sport coats. One of the men was in the middle bench seat. He reached out, grabbed Michael's hand, and pulled him into the center. The man with the sport coat took it off, threw it into the back luggage space, and jumped in, sandwiching Michael in the middle. The SUV immediately took off.

Rudy twisted himself around from the passenger side of the front seat to look back at Michael. "We got a report that your Aunt Mildred stubbed her toe. So I thought that warranted calling out special forces from Camp Pendleton to help," Rudy said, laughing at his own joke.

Michael was a little too dazed to give even a courtesy laugh.

Suddenly the men on either side of Michael grabbed his arms and pulled them back. A man in the far backseat slid a flak jacket over his arms and fastened it on.

"Do you know where we're going?" asked Rudy.

"Yes, to some old bunker on Aliso Hill."

"Hey, you're a smart bloke. The FBI guys took a long time to figure that out."

Michael wanted to ask Rudy who he was but thought he might

have more success starting with the soldiers. He turned to his left and right and asked, "Are you two Marines from Camp Pendleton?"

The Marine who greeted him on campus said, "Sorry, sir, we're not at liberty to disclose any information." His accent revealed that he was from no further "down under" than Sydney, Nebraska.

"That really wasn't a very clever disguise you had on," said Michael. "Did you design that, Rudy?"

"Well, we do what we can in a pinch. Thought it best not to put a combat-ready soldier on campus to get you," said Rudy.

"Who are you exactly?" Michael asked.

"Well, I can't give you my real name, but I really am from Australian Intelligence. I'm now officially on loan to the CIA for the current operation."

"Would it do any good to ask you for ID?"

"The fact that you asked means you know it wouldn't. You've probably seen enough movies to know that we spooks have a whole gaggle of IDs stashed away in Swiss lockboxes and such." Rudy laughed.

Michael had warmed up enough to at least smile this time.

"Why was the FBI asking me questions about you?" asked Michael.

"I dunno," said Rudy. "Your agencies are supposed to be cooperating—guess they're still learning how. But you'll be seeing Schofield and Lister in a tic. We're almost there."

Michael still had a small amount of paranoia that the soldiers in the car might be only posing as Marines. But when Rudy mentioned the names of the FBI agents, the doubts subsided.

"What do you want me to do?" Michael asked.

"The guys in charge didn't authorize me to give a full briefing. I suppose they'll do that when we get to the command post. But how's your Badui?" Rudy said, smiling and giving an obvious hint.

"Why is ASIS involved in this?" Michael asked, not expecting an answer. But Rudy surprised him.

"I've been working Indonesian terror cells since the Bali bombings. My people thought I could help out with your little problem here in Laguna. Oh, so sorry I stood you up on Friday. I had to take a quick trip to a gem of a place called Prescott, Arizona. Delightful."

They drove up the road leading to Aliso Park. A gate that blocked the road at night was pulled across the road with a sign that said Park Closed. Another dark SUV was parked just behind the gate on the side of the road. A soldier in fatigues jumped out as Michael's vehicle approached. The man unlocked the gate, pulled it open, and waved them through.

As Michael passed the SUV, he could see several armed soldiers through the vehicle's open door. He also saw agents Schofield and Lister walking to their sedan. Michael was hoping to talk with them at least briefly. But their "package" had been delivered safely, and it was time for them to go. Schofield obviously wouldn't be returning Michael's phone call.

Michael's SUV drove into the parking lot, over the curb, and behind a cinder block restroom building, where they found two other SUVs and two large utility vans. About a dozen Marines in fatigues were sitting in the shade with painted faces and a range of weapons and equipment laying on tarps in front of them.

The soldiers in the SUV walked Michael to one of the large utility vans. It had a variety of antennas on top. The side and back doors were wide open. A middle-aged man in a Navy uniform was sitting at a console inside and saw Michael coming. He peeled off his headphones and jumped outside the van, waving for Michael to run to him. His Marine escort saw it too and pushed Michael along faster.

The Navy man said in a loud whisper, "Quick, it's almost time," and shoved the headphones onto Michael's head and held up his hands to keep everyone quiet.

Michael was trying to catch his breath and listen carefully at the same time by gulping in air and letting it out as quietly as he could. All he heard was a very soft static. The Navy man was looking carefully at his watch while he raised his other hand. He looked over at the other utility van with more antennas on top. He dropped his hand in karate chop motion, and the soft static in Michael's ears disappeared at the same moment. The crisp silence in the headphones was like a sensory deprivation chamber for the ears. Michael's breathing was getting back to normal in the minute that followed. He sat down in the van. He didn't know yet what he was listening for. The Navy officer shoved a clipboard with paper and pen into Michael's hand with no comment.

The silence ended abruptly when he heard a slight hiss—a microphone was being keyed, but there was no voice yet. Then a pathetic sound broke in. The audio equipment was so good that Michael could hear every strain, quiver, and vibration in the weak, struggling voice. He grabbed the pen from the clipboard and started writing. The transmission was from a native Badui speaker. Michael translated on the fly.

"My angel, speak. Shall I light the lamp? My angel, speak. Shall I light…"

The stark silence fell back into the headphones for a moment. Then the hiss of a keyed mic returned, and then the voice. "Shall I light it now?"

Silence fell again and this time stayed. Michael waited. When the radio man saw he wasn't writing anymore, he pulled the headphones off of Michael and put one side to his own ear. Then he started making a thumbs-up motion to the other van. They gave him an okay sign back.

Michael handed the man the clipboard with his barely legible translation. The Navy man read it, quickly scribbled a note of his own on the bottom of the page, and handed it to a soldier in fatigues waiting to help.

"This confirms it. Use a secure line to relay this to the Pentagon right now. Let me know the moment they acknowledge receipt." He turned to Michael. "Sorry for pulling those things off your head. We've been jamming this frequency so the guy can't receive any 'go' signal from his people. We turn it off to hear his half-hourly message but fire it right back up again."

"It's okay," Michael said.

"My name's Commander Sessions of Naval Intelligence. I'm in charge of the information gathering and communications. Here's the situation; listen very carefully. We believe we have one or two young Indonesian Muslims in the pillbox a hundred fifty meters away—on top of that ridge," he said, pointing to a small rise above the park.

"We believe they have enough ammonium nitrate to atomize the top of Aliso Hill and are religiously motivated to pull the trigger. We believe they have enough cesium-137 attached to the bomb to kill hundreds or thousands and render the city and surrounding areas uninhabitable for fifty years. We believe they're waiting for a signal in this Badui language to launch the suicide attack—your translation just now seems to confirm that. We believe they may have been hiding up here for as long as two weeks. We've been in position only since six this morning. We believe they don't know we're here. We believe their radiation containment is breaking down; our readings have been rising significantly since we arrived. Please do not waste our time asking questions or making suggestions about assaults, tunnels, poison gas, or air strikes. We already know every option, we have several plans, and we're waiting for orders. Do you understand?"

"Yes, sir," Michael answered. The "sir" just popped out, programming from his time in the military.

"Good. We have you here for one reason: to help us with that weird language. You with me?"

"Yes, sir," said Michael.

Michael was overcome by the gravity of the situation. Commander Sessions was a barely controlled basket case. One side of his face was twitching while he spoke. The stress for everyone there was palpable.

Michael's mind was racing to put together the pieces. They couldn't evacuate the city because that might alert the terrorists that they knew an attack was coming. They couldn't blow up the pillbox because of the cesium. They could only hide a tiny military presence just down the hill. They had just enough personnel to attempt a SWAT-style assault on the bunker, but that was obviously a plan of last resort. How hard could it be for a terrorist to push a button if he detected an attack? One thought seemed to hover above all the rest: If the bomb goes off, no one on Aliso Hill right now will survive. This was a literal do-or-die mission for those involved.

Michael sat down on the ground behind the van and prayed. He asked God to spare these brave men and to guard the people in the city below, who were walking around with no idea their lives were hanging in the balance. "Lord, everything I have is yours. You know that I haven't withheld anything from you. Empty my cup and fill it with courage from above. Don't let me wilt. Help me to stand strong with these brave men and do my job."

Michael put a cigarette in his mouth but couldn't find his lighter after patting down every pocket. He noticed a couple of Marines smoking at a picnic table in the shade, and he went over and asked for a light. A young soldier who looked a lot like Darren Stevens, except with a blond crew cut instead of surfer locks, tossed Michael a book of matches and said, "I hope I get a chance to ask for those back."

Suddenly a man also in fatigues and face paint but at least twice the age of the soldiers sitting in the shade walked toward them, holding several sheets of paper. "Gentlemen, please gather in close; we have some new photos from recon." He sat down at the picnic table so the men could look over his shoulder.

Michael noticed the silver oak leaf—a lieutenant colonel, probably the leader of a special forces unit and obviously the commander of this assault. Michael couldn't see the photos, but he could hear the whole briefing. No one was making any effort to keep information from him anymore. What he knew didn't matter now.

"See this line in the concrete? We're pretty certain this is a large Styrofoam plug covering the entrance they cut into the side of the bunker—the only way in, the only way out. We don't think they'd risk a booby trap in that closed space. They want to be alive and alert to carry out their mission. They may have rigged some kind of alarm though. Also, looks like hot emissions are still increasing. We go in with gas masks. You get any of that cesium in your lungs and it'll cook you from the inside. You won't keel over immediately, but you'll be the walking dead."

The briefing continued as they went over attack plans and contingencies. As Michael listened, fears from his Vietnam experience began to wash over him. He almost yelled when a hand suddenly grabbed his shoulder. He turned and saw Commander Sessions.

"Come with me."

Michael followed him back to the radio van.

"The planners at the Pentagon want to know if you can speak Badui well enough on the radio to make the Indonesians think you're this angel they're listening for."

"If he's expecting to hear a native speaker, I don't have enough practice speaking it to fool him. Maybe if it's garbled somewhat. You know, if there could be static or interference to mask my accent or something," Michael said.

"Oh, baby," said Commander Sessions, patting the side of the van. "We can add echo chambers, reverb, static, backup singers, anything you want. We just need to distract them for at least forty seconds."

"If we can distort the transmission, I think I can do it," said Michael.

"They may demand a code word from you to verify you're the real contact. The job is to keep them occupied communicating with you for the full forty seconds."

"I got it, Commander."

"Okay then. We're gonna send you up with the assault team so you can see what's going on. You'll have a hand-held transmitter. We'll be adding the distortion from the van. They'll plant you just behind the ridgeline with the larger group. We're only sending three men inside. Lieutenant Colonel Gonzalez will be in charge. He'll go over the details with you," Sessions said.

Michael worked with Sessions and a technician to get the radio interference just right and tested it on another frequency. They put a helmet on Michael and cinched down his flak jacket. Then they gave him what looked like a fancy walkie-talkie with an earpiece connected and sent him over to Lieutenant Colonel Gonzalez.

As Michael approached, five of the men were kneeling in front of a chaplain with helmets off to take communion before the mission. He was looking at the backs of their crew-cut heads and was stunned how each one reminded him of the prodigal son in Rembrandt's painting.

Gonzalez grabbed Michael by the flak jacket, pulled him aside, and carefully explained his role. He sternly reminded Michael that the lives of his men were in the balance. Michael didn't need to be reminded. Lieutenant Colonel Gonzalez's facial scars revealed that he had seen a lot of action. The Pentagon had probably called on the most experienced special-forces leader they could put on scene quickly.

Gonzalez assembled the men and walked them through the operation, including Michael's role, one last time. The timing had to be perfect, and they had no more time to rehearse. They had to make the raid at the top of the hour, when the next broadcast from the bunker took place. The president himself had given the green light.

Working with the Pentagon, the commanders had cobbled together a sixty-second script for Michael to translate and broadcast. He had been practicing every moment that someone was not giving him new instructions.

Gonzalez said, "Let's go," and the Marines walked up a small dirt road for about twenty yards and then waded through coastal scrub on steep, uneven terrain where the road had been bulldozed by city leaders years ago.

There was no talking after leaving the park. Gonzalez was using hand motions to position his people. Three of them with gas masks were very slowly moving as close to the bunker as possible. Michael had heard the last rehearsal of the plan. They had to get inside and manage clean, fast kill shots of everyone in there without hitting any of the explosives—or overpower and knife anyone within reach. No grenades for obvious reasons. They were carrying several kinds of weapons, including what looked like a military version of a sawed-off shotgun. The men were wearing darkened goggles that they could flip off as they entered the darkened bunker. No time to wait for pupils to dilate.

During the final walk-through, Gonzalez was sounding optimistic to his men. When Michael saw the pillbox, he thought Gonzalez was simply trying to make an impossible situation sound possible. If someone inside simply needed to push a button, the assault seemed a long shot.

The support team took up positions by lying down along a berm where the hill leveled off at the top. Gonzalez and his sergeant major had earpieces and were listening for orders from the command post in the park below.

The three-man assault team was in position. They gave a hand signal that they were ready. Gonzalez acknowledged it by signaling back. Michael knew all the sign language from his time in the military—it hadn't changed.

The sound in Michael's earpiece abruptly changed from soft-white noise to crisp silence. The frequency jammer had been shut down as planned. Michael was to wait for the Badui transmission and then, upon Gonzalez's signal, begin reading the script in Badui.

On schedule, a voice came up on the frequency. The voice sounded even more pathetic than before. The breathing was labored. There were gasps and wheezes between words. This guy did not sound in good shape—the radiation was taking its toll.

"My angel, speak."

There was a pause that seemed to go on forever. Michael was trying to think what he should do if he didn't say anything else. Should he break in and start the script? *God, help me,* he prayed.

Finally, another brief transmission.

"My angel, speak."

The young Indonesian man had finished, and the crisp silence returned.

Gonzalez gave the signal and Michael read the first line of the Badui script into the transmitter. At the same time, the intentional static was added to the broadcast.

"Your angel is here, but we must wait a little longer."

Michael let go of the transmit button very briefly to listen for a response before reading further.

Suddenly, the frequency lit up. Michael was lying on his stomach behind the berm, looking at the bunker entrance, and then quickly rolled on to his back as he listened intently to the weak voice mustering strength to cry out into the radio. In a sudden burst of hope and dread, the man began speaking quickly and with strange breathing patterns. It took every ounce of concentration Michael could muster to try to understand what the man was saying.

"Oh, my angel, you have come. Finally you have come. I cannot go on. I have failed God. I have failed my people. My brother is dead. I too am dead. May I light the lamp and die?"

Michael keyed the mic connected to the small radio on his belt and departed from the script. "No, you must not light the lamp yet!"

Michael leaped to his feet at the same moment Gonzalez was giving the signal to attack. Michael held his arm up at a right angle with a clenched fist. Everyone there stopped in their tracks at the sign to freeze. He had enough turns as patrol leader in Vietnam to make the sign with authority.

He began walking toward the bunker entrance while talking on the radio.

"My brother, I am sending you a trusted helper right now to carry your burdens for you," Michael said in Badui.

"I am now alone. Yes, please send a helper," the young man gasped.

"He is arriving now. You will know him by his blue jacket, and he will be smoking a cigarette. He will speak to you in Indonesian and then in English. That is how you will know the angel has sent him."

"Yes, bring cigarettes," the man's words were slurring, and he sounded nearly delirious.

Scrambling for what to do, Gonzalez had his sergeant major, one of the best marksmen in the Corps, pick up a sniper rifle with a silencer. He had it trained right at an exposed part of the back of Michael's neck. Did the translator go rogue? Either way, he was putting everyone in immediate peril.

Michael suddenly gave the Marine sniper a bigger target when he unexpectedly took off his helmet and flak jacket.

Gonzalez had his hand up in the freeze signal, but it was starting to shake almost violently. He couldn't give the go ahead to shoot Michael because the bullet would go right through him and hit the side of the bunker. One of the three men near the bunker entrance had a knife out, ready to take Michael down silently. Gonzalez kept his hand in the freeze position. Something about Michael's own hand signal urged Gonzalez to trust. He knew Michael must be a former soldier and wouldn't do anything mad to get them all killed. What was he hearing in Badui?

When he had his flak jacket off, Michael pulled out a cigarette and lit it. Then, speaking into the radio, he said, "Your cigarettes are now there with my trusted helper. He will be coming in to bear your burdens. Greet him warmly."

Michael was able to get his fingers under a crease in the Styrofoam. He gave it a pull, and the block pulled out easily. Michael immediately blew smoke through the entrance and then spoke in Indonesian, a language in which he was much more experienced. "Hello, my friend. The angel sent me to help." Michael repeated it in English and then crawled through the opening.

The stench inside was unbearable—diesel fuel, rotting flesh and food, and human waste littered the space. Light was pouring into one corner of the bunker through the opening he had just uncorked. The barrels of explosives stuffed inside left very little room to maneuver.

Michael had to wait a moment for his eyes to adjust to see to the far corner. A man was lying on the ground next to a small pile of wadded-up blankets, spilled food cans, and empty water jugs. On some cinder blocks next to him were a radio, a hand-crank generator, and several car batteries. He wasn't moving. Michael thought he was probably recovering from the exertion of talking on the radio moments ago.

"I lit a cigarette for you," Michael said in Indonesian, thinking that would be the most familiar language to put the man at ease. He reached down and held the cigarette to the man's mouth, and the man was able to take a small drag on it. All the while, Michael was looking in the darkness of the corner for wires, buttons, keys... anything that might be a bomb trigger.

Then he saw it. Right next to the man's left hand was a remote for a garage door opener, duct taped to the wall of the bunker, inches above the ground. The man could easily hit the square red button with one quick flip of his wrist.

Michael got on his knees next to the man and gave him another puff on the cigarette. He touched the man's forehead and said, again in Indonesian, "God has sent me to you to care for you in your last hours. I have a pack of cigarettes and matches. I'll leave them here with you."

Michael then leaned over the man, who had been stewing in his own filth for days, and set the cigarettes near his left elbow. He lowered himself across the man's torso, slowly putting all his weight on the man's body and firmly grabbing the man's left wrist. The man could barely move in his weakened condition, and Michael very gently and quietly loosened the duct tape with his free hand. He then stood up and set the device on an old window ledge.

"What's your name?" Michael asked the man in English. He was afraid to ask before he found the trigger in case the man expected him to know his name.

In English he replied, "Can I have the cigarette?"

Then Michael said, "Yes, yes you can have the cigarette."

He then keyed the mic of the radio that he had stuffed in his pocket and said in a strong but gentle voice, "I have the lamp. All is well, my friend, all is well." He hoped that Gonzalez's radioman would get the message: *Don't attack!*

Michael put the cigarette in the man's mouth, and he clutched it in his lips. Michael saw sores all over the man's face and neck behind the matted long hair and beard growth.

After a couple of puffs the man said, "Wijaya. My name is Wijaya."

"That means victory," said Michael.

Tears suddenly gushed from his eyes. "My younger brother is dead. I buried him two days ago," Wijaya said in strained English, turning his head to look at a mound of dirt in the other corner of the bunker.

Michael realized he must have buried him right there, but not deep enough to keep the putrid smell of death from wafting up. What a horrific hell hole this was for Wijaya.

"I have failed God and everyone," said Wijaya.

Michael quickly found some water, lifted Wijaya's head, and gave him a drink.

After a few more puffs on the cigarette, nicotine reached the young man's bloodstream, and he seemed suddenly to become more aware of his surroundings. *Who is this man? The mission!*

Light the lamp! Wijaya began to stir and pushed himself up to his hands and knees. As he moved, he became more conscious of Michael and what had just occurred. He got on one knee and then to his feet—a Herculean effort for a man nearly dead from radiation poisoning. Michael stood up as quickly as a slightly arthritic, pudgy, middle-aged college professor could manage in order to put himself between Wijaya and the bomb trigger.

Wijaya lunged at the trigger as if to go right through Michael to grab it. Michael, who weighed almost twice as much as the rail-thin Indonesian, caught him like he was giving him a bear hug. Michael then stumbled on the bedroll at his feet and fell face-first, holding Wijaya tightly. A loud pop echoed through the bunker. Wijaya went limp, and Michael cautiously loosened his grip and pushed away from the young man. He had landed on top of Wijaya with full force, and the vertebrae in the center of Wijaya's neck shattered when he hit the corner of one of the car batteries.

In the dim light, Michael looked closely at Wijaya and could see his eyes were open and he was still breathing. He saw drops of blood hitting Wijaya's face and touched his own lip, which split open when he slammed into Wijaya's forehead.

Michael picked up the conscious but completely paralyzed man and carried him to the entrance of the pillbox. He crawled out, gave the all clear signal, and then pulled Wijaya outside the bunker and laid him down in the sun and fresh coastal air. Michael sat down next to him and held Wijaya's head in his lap. He stroked his matted hair and recited the story of the prodigal son in Indonesian as the man's life slowly ebbed away.

On the order of Lieutenant Colonel Gonzalez, none of the Marines rushed forward to help. They were all behind the berm with gas masks on. The radiation readings were now deadly.

FIFTEEN

"You'd think they'd have a special radiation unit at some hospital in Laguna County," Reagan said as she got out of Darren's station wagon. He called it a vintage wagon, but there was nothing vintage about it. It was just an old heap with a surfboard rack on the top.

"I thought traffic to downtown Los Angeles would be lighter on a Saturday morning," said Charlene.

"No, in L.A., Saturday morning is about as bad as any weekday now," Darren said as he parked next to a row of TV news vans with satellite dishes on top. "Look at all the news guys. Hey, maybe they'll want a word from one of Dr. J.'s students."

"This is a really ugly hospital. You'd think they'd find a better place to take care of a national hero. So who else is coming?" asked Reagan.

"After the final on Thursday, almost everybody said they were coming to visit this morning," said Darren.

"Should we wait for them out here in the parking lot?" Reagan asked.

"Nah, they'll find his room. Let's just go in," Darren replied.

They asked at the front desk about visiting the radiation contamination unit.

"I'm sure you're here to see Michael Jernigan like everyone else. Are you media, friends, or well-wishers?" asked the receptionist.

The three of them looked at each other and then said, "Friends."

The receptionist said, "Good answer, because Dr. Jernigan has requested only friends today. The media has been swarming all week, and grateful people from Laguna have been coming in constantly."

They gave their names and discovered they were on the list to visit. The receptionist gave them special visitor's badges and sent them to an elevator that took them two floors below ground level. They wound around a few corridors, following the signs to the unit. Rounding a corner, they were shocked to see a long hallway packed with solemn people standing quietly. Some were praying, others seemed just to be waiting, and still others were sitting on the floor as if they had been there awhile. A sign hanging from the ceiling said RADIATION CONTAMINATION UNIT: AUTHORIZATION REQUIRED FOR ENTRY.

Darren whispered to Charlene while pointing not so politely, "Dude, look at that."

They saw about a dozen Buddhist monks with shaved heads, sandals, and colorful robes standing together. Behind them were a group of young men with very short hair—Marines who were grateful to Michael for getting them off Aliso Hill in one piece. One of them, if he got a chance, was going to ask Michael to give him his book of matches back. The rest of the crowd looked like people from Michael's church, neighbors, or colleagues from San Gabriel College. Willa Lightner and Frieda were there with the new baby, who was sleeping in a sling over Frieda's shoulder.

Reagan whispered, "Hey, there's Virginia," and waved at her. She also spotted Gyandev, who was sitting on the floor against a wall with his head in his hands.

Virginia walked over to see them. She said a nurse had just been out to brief the group that had been gathering.

"We're standing right in front of a window to Michael's room. Several times a day they draw back some lead-lined shutters so visitors can interact with him. You can use a microphone to talk to him. But the nurse said he really can't talk, so it's frustrating for him. The nerves to his vocal cords are severely damaged. She listed some other things that were wrong, too, like terrible sores all over his body. But she said he actually feels better today. The first few days after his radiation exposure were his worst. Constant nausea and vomiting and cramps, no eating. I hear he looks emaciated. But she said he's in the latent stage, which can last for a day or two, when radiation patients generally feel better."

"So he's getting better?" asked Reagan.

"Oh no, dear," said Virginia. "He's almost certainly going to die. Didn't you know?"

They all knew from the news reports that this was a possibility, but it just hadn't sunk in. They were holding on to the hope that with the right care and treatment he would make it.

Virginia continued, "The nurse said he has the worst type of acute radiation syndrome, and his body is deteriorating very quickly. The dear man is radioactive."

"When will we get to see him?" asked Charlene.

"The nurse said they'll slide back the shutters at ten o'clock. Oh, I've got something for you all," said Virginia.

She had a shopping bag in her hand. She set it down and pulled out three copies of a small book.

"I paid some graphic arts students at school to typeset and print some copies of Dr. Jernigan's translation of *The Five Crossings*. Didn't they do a good job? Gyandev wants to try to get it into the hands of a national publishing house. But I wanted to get one to all his students right away."

Charlene marveled at the cover. The students worked with a clear photograph of the aging original but were able to bring the colors and details back to life in a very sharp reproduction. The pages of text were formatted like poetry, and everything about it was a work of art. They all thanked Virginia profusely.

"It's five minutes till ten. Let's get set up," said Reagan.

They unrolled a banner they had carried in, pulled some other things out of a bag, and squeezed into the crowded hallway.

The nurse, covered head to toe in a special disposable gown

and wearing a filtering mask, came in to ask Michael if he wished to greet the visitors who had come to see him.

He nodded yes.

She helped him drink some water through a straw, something he had been unable to do until today, and then combed his hair and spruced up his bed for him. She also put the microphone in front of his mouth in case he wanted to try to talk.

As the nurse was leaving, she hit a button that rolled the shutters open slowly from left to right across a long panel of windows around the room.

Michael pushed the button that moved the bed into a more upright position.

The first thing he saw was Charlene holding up a red robe. She was fighting back tears as she saw him in such terrible condition.

Then the shutters rolled back to reveal Reagan holding a gold ring and a pair of sandals.

Next was Darren, smiling from ear to ear and holding a big roast beef sandwich and an extra-large soda.

Michael was catching on to the theme. The next thing he saw was Virginia and Gyandev holding up a large print of his favorite Rembrandt. He recalled his favorite passages from the story: "Quick! Bring the best robe and put it on him. Put a ring on his finger and sandals on his feet. Bring the fattened calf and kill it. Let's have a feast and celebrate. For this son of mine was dead and is alive again; he was lost and is found. So they began to celebrate."

As the shutters rolled past the last panel of glass, Michael saw a banner with bold letters: YOU'RE AMERICA'S MAP NUTH!

Michael pulled the microphone close to his lips, and silence fell in the hallway in anticipation. He swallowed hard between every word, but he was able to say, "Promise…me…you'll…tell…the…Cardamom…people…this…story."

Darren grabbed the microphone in the hallway and said, "You bet, Dr. J. I'm going to visit the Cardamom and surf Thailand for you."

After a few minutes of awkward gawking and sad waving, the shutters began to roll closed.

Reagan asked her friends, every one of whom was wiping away tears, "Is he going to die alone in that room?"

"Impossible," Gyandev said. "Our eyes deceive us. I'm certain he is never really alone. The one who transcends boundaries is with him always."

It's a Harsh,

Crazy,

Beautiful,

Messed Up,

Breathtaking

World...

And People Are Talking About It...